YOU'RE THE GREATEST

GREATEST

HOW VALIDATED EMPLOYEES
CAN IMPACT YOUR BOTTOM LINE

FRANK MAGUIRE

WITH STEVE WILLIFORD

YOU'RE THE GREATEST

GREATEST

HOW VALIDATED EMPLOYEES
CAN IMPACT YOUR BOTTOM LINE

Frank Maguire
32123 Lindero Canyon Road Suite #204
Westlake Village, CA 91361
(818) 889 8086
E-mail: info@maguirecommunications.com

Editor-in-Chief	Steve Williford
Associate Editor	Akbar Alikhan
Cover Design	Barry Burns & Jamie Mattock
Cover Photography	Charis Portaiture

Publisher	Flow Motion Inc.
	P.O. Box 379024 Las Vegas, NV 89137
	888-818-FLOW www.FlowMotionInc.com

Library of Congress Cataloging-in-Publication Data

Maguire, Frank and Williford, Steve
You're the Greatest:
How Validated Employees Can Impact Your Bottom
Line / Frank Maguire and Steve Williford
p. cm.
ISBN 0-9765607-0-4
I. Business   I. Title

━━ · YOU'RE THE GREATEST! · ━━

ACKNOWLEDGEMENTS

Before we start on our journey through the pages of this book let me express my gratitude to a few of those individuals who encouraged and supported me as I agonized over the many details and doubts that entered my mind during the writing process. I say a few because it is impossible to include them all. We have all experienced acts of generosity from people, some of whom we have forgotten. These individuals have been there for me all the way and indeed have helped make this book possible.

First and foremost, there is my friend and co-author Steve Williford. Simply stated, without his support, there would be no book! Steve listened to me talk about this dream for years and finally offered to assist me and drove the project to completion. Thank you Steve for making my dream come true. You are truly a talented and gifted writer and friend.

I also want to thank my long time friends Charles Osgood and Ted Koppel. Although they probably don't know it, their success has validated me during the moments of self doubt through the years. Thanks guys. You done good!

My old boss Fred Smith also left a lasting impression on me. He is a true leader and gave me the opportunity to help create a corporate culture at FedEx that has been a beacon of light throughout corporate America. Fred you are a CEO's CEO! Every employee of FedEx and their families owe you a debt of gratitude.

Then there's Harry Keenan, and John Culkin. The two brothers I never had. There are no words to describe their role in helping me hang on when I thought all was lost. They're both gone now but I still talk to them on a daily basis.

And last but not least my friends John and Geri Cusenza, who opened both their hearts and home to me in beautiful Hidden Valley, California and gave me a spiritual sanctuary to gather my thoughts and put them on paper. I have never experienced a more tranquil and spiritual place where the mind and body co-exist as a whole. I know now where God lives! Thank you John and Geri for your support and encouragement.

And now on with the journey!

CONTENTS

INTRODUCTION

Thank you for taking your precious time to read this book. I hope it will have an impact on your life. In the 40 odd years that I've been in the corporate arena, I have had a great number of experiences. I like to tell my audiences, "I have chronological credibility."

I hope that you will be able to use what I am going to discuss with you, in ways that will enhance your personal life, your business life, and, in addition, increase your bottom line. I have found from my experiences that when you take care of your employees, your company is more profitable. I want you to understand the connection between validated employees and profits. Looked at this way, your bottom line then becomes an invaluable measure of your success.

So this is a bottom line book, presented in an unconventional way, from one who was there in the early days of Federal Express Corporation, American Broadcasting Corporation, KFC, American Airlines, I was involved in growing and nurturing businesses back then, and I'm still doing that every day. I'm going to tell you about things that I've seen, done, and learned. I'm going to prove how a highly motivated and dedicated work force impacts the bottom line.

In the years that I have toiled in the trenches of corporate America, I have witnessed never-ending search for the secret formula that would open the vaults of productivity, customer satisfaction, and employee morale.

We've tried everything on the menu. Remember MBO, Zero-Based Budget, Just In Time Inventory, Balanced Scorecard, Quality Circles, Statistical Process Control, TQM, ISO 2000, and Six Sigma? We discovered that we still had problems even after we improved our quality, reduced our overhead and increased our cycle time. Over time, the remedies changed, but the problems did not.

We are certainly experiencing change. Change in technology, the new economy, mergers and acquisitions, downsizing and reengineering, and outsourcing. The transforming of corporate America is a direct result of the changes occurring all around us. These changes aren't going away. They are here and they are now.

Here's another change. Most of our very wealthy CEOs are under 40 years old. Guess what they're worried about? Turnover, how to create and maintain a highly dedicated and motivated workforce, skippers, the people who come, stay for a few years, and leave.

Even though I don't know you, I have a high regard for who you are. As a matter of fact, I think you're the greatest. I'll explain a little further down the path, but the important thing is how you feel about yourself. The truth of the matter is you are the greatest friend and companion you ever had.

Do you believe that?
Do you accept that?

If you haven't even considered these questions, you better learn to, because it will have a great impact on your bottom line.

You're the Greatest

That's my bottom line. I don't even know you, yet I think you're the greatest. I don't have to know you, to know that about you. If you don't think that about yourself, you must learn.

Here's why that's important to business. When you accept that concept about yourself and others, you make more money. Your self perception determines your future. People end up being who they think they are. In many ways, life is a self-fulfilling prophecy.

I'm past the 60 yard line now, and I can tell you that my life has definitely been affected by how I felt about myself. If you don't feel very positive about yourself, you're going to have a hard time feeling that way about others, not to the extent that they deserve. That means you short change those who are most important to you, from your spouse to your employees.

If you are shortchanging yourself, that means you see others as you are, not as they are. So, if you don't have the self-esteem you need, you won't be able to see those qualities in the people around you.

I've come to realize who I am, a lover of people, a husband, a father, a friend who has his share of faults, but a loyal friend to many. I'm a dreamer; I'm imaginative; I'm musical; I communicate well; I invest emotionally; I make people feel good about themselves.

My weaknesses? Very simple. Don't put me in charge of your accounts receivable or payable departments. I'm not a technically analytical person. I don't enjoy confrontation. If I had a chance to look in the rearview mirror, I'd do a lot of things differently.

In the book, The Little Prince, the fox came out of the forest and said to the little prince, "It is only with the heart that one can see clearly. What is essential is invisible to the eye."

What is essential about us is not the car we drive, the suit we wear, the money in the bank or the size of our house. What defines us is the light behind our eyes.

In other words, I have strengths, I have weaknesses, but this is who I am, and until I accept and like myself right where I am, I will not enjoy life nor will I enjoy my journey. *And to the extent I accept and like myself determines how effectively I can help anyone else along the way, personally or professionally.* You can't fake it.

That doesn't mean you won't have moments of anxiety or doubt, everybody does. Great companies are the result of people who feel good about themselves, with total self-confidence, grace, and dignity, which is not to be confused with arrogance. Being the greatest, among other things, means being able to obtain a measure of happiness, come what may, instead of walking around being bitter or angry in the face of frustration or adversity. I call it the "attitude of gratitude." It's the ability to get up in the morning and be grateful to be alive.

I have been around a lot of companies and I've seen what makes them grow. Those who thrive, take care of themselves and their employees. It doesn't happen by accident. The attitude of gratitude requires time, attention, and cultivation.

My goal is turn up your rheostat, and help make your light shine a little brighter. I love to play on my piano along with that great spiritual song, This Little Light of Mine.

This little light of mine. I'm going to let it shine.
This little light of mine. I'm going to let it shine.
This little light of mine. I'm going to let it shine.
Let it shine. Let it shine. Let it shine.

Whether it is a philosophy, or whether it is joyful, you get to decide. So many of us are in distress, and I want to help you decide not to live there and not to allow your employees to live there.

My objective in this book is to help you understand that you are the greatest! Period.

I want you to understand the importance and impact of that accomplishment. Forget business plans, quotas, goals, quality standards, mission statements, etc. It begins in here. If you don't have it "in here," none of the other stuff matters. On the contrary, if you do have it, you'll make everything you do sing, and you will make more money.

You want a motivated work force? You want high productivity? You want low turnover? You want increased revenues? This style of management achieves all of that and lets you look forward to Monday morning, laugh during the day, and sleep like a baby at night.

It's time your ticket got punched. Find a seat. We're leaving the station. Let's take this journey together. Welcome aboard!

Frank Maguire

YOU'RE THE GREATEST

· CHAPTER ONE ·

TELL ME
ONE MORE TIME

**"PEOPLE WILL NEVER FORGET HOW
YOU MADE THEM FEEL."**

Effective communication can dramatically affect the productivity of your company and the careers of your employees! Even the most casual comment made by an employer to one of the employees can have a major impact on that employee's performance. Depending upon the particular employee, it may even energize the whole corporation.

A Case In Point

You never know how your behavior affects those around you. In fact, it could take 40 years to find out! Let me tell you a story as we begin our journey.

About 40 years ago, a good friend of mine, Jim Harriott who worked with me at ABC, asked me to interview a young man right out of college for a job on the staff of a new program called Flair Reports. I said, "Jim, I'm leaving for the weekend, and I still have some things to do." But Jim was persistent. "Frank, I'd appreciate it if you do this for me." I then agreed, "Okay. Tell him to come on over."

I remember well this 23 year-old young man from London who walked into my office at the American Broadcasting Corporation to apply for a job. He was working as a copy boy at a rock-and-roll radio station in New York City. His job was to tear off the wire copy and bring it to the disc jockeys who would read the news. We called it "rip and read" in those days.

The first thing I noticed was this young man had a light in his eyes, and called me, "Mr. Maguire." As we talked, I sensed that he had a special quality about him, and I told him I would schedule an audition for him the following week. He seemed pleased with that, thanked me and left. When I returned to my office Monday morning, I found an audition tape on my desk with a note from Ted. He was so determined to make the team that over the weekend, he had produced his own audition tape. That's what they mean by "fire in the belly."

To this day, I have a copy of the tape in my files. It was a live interview from the scene of a Nazi Party rally in Yorktown, on the upper east side of New York City, with the ominous sounds of goose steps in the background. You could tell immediately that Ted's presence was not welcomed. He was hassled and called a troublemaker. Finally, he said to one of the militant leaders that he would agree to turn off his microphone and leave, but he had one last question.

"All right, one question," the man said.

Ted asked, "Could you please tell me who is the president of the United States?" There followed a long pause. Then the man shouted, "You see, you're just trying to make trouble. You're just a troublemaker."

With the sounds of growing dissent and the ever present goose steps in the background, I can still hear Ted's final words . . . "This is Ted Koppel for ABC News."

I pushed the stop button on my tape machine. I knew he had what I was looking for. He showed me that he understood that we were transitioning from the old rip-and-read reporting to using the dramatic impact of sound and words. Radio was about to become a visual medium.

There were many other qualified, older, and more experienced candidates. On paper, his chances were slim to none. The difference was, he really wanted the job. He called me every day, and he did it in a very diplomatic way, which isn't easy when you're pursuing your dream. He didn't bug me. He would say, "Mr. Maguire? This is Ted Koppel. I just wanted to call and find out. You told me you were going to be making the decision this week. I really want the job. Am I still a candidate?"

I didn't make that decision for about three weeks. During that time, I received many calls from young Ted Koppel. Guess how many calls I received from the other candidates? None. Like so many of us, they just waited for me to call them. The more I talked to Ted, the more I liked him, and I knew he had something special to offer all of us. You know now who I hired.

There's a lesson for all of us in the story.

Ted Koppel showed me a solution to that limbo we all find ourselves in from time to time. He did something. He didn't just wait by the phone, with his heart in his throat. He took action, even though he must have known how high the cards were stacked against him. You can do that when you feel good about yourself. After all, what's the worst that could happen? He wouldn't get the job. At least he would have gone down swinging.

So many times, you hear people say, "I'm waiting for them to call me back," but Ted made it very clear to me that he wanted that job.

The next time you wonder whether your initial meeting went well or whether they have decided to use your product or service, don't wait for them to call you. Pick up the phone and call them. Nobody is ever going to be offended that you want the job or the order. The "prize" will usually go to the person who wants it the most. . . and takes action!

Would I Be Remembered as the Person Who Fired Ted Koppel?

Here was Ted Koppel, twenty-three years old with no experience. My boss called me into his office for one of those unscheduled meetings, and asked, "Frank, how long you been around here?"

"About six months, Bob." I had no idea where he was

going. "Somebody just told me you hired a 23-year-old kid for the network — with absolutely no experience."

I could feel the sweat begin to drip down my back.

I said, "Yeah. He's very good. His name is Ted Koppel. He's really got a great talent."

He said, "Well, that's great. I'm glad. Then he'll have no trouble finding another job. Fire him. We're running a network here, not a daycare center."

Wow. He didn't ask me to fire Ted. He didn't suggest that I fire him. He told me to fire him. Since I was not exactly the pillar upon which ABC Radio was built, I knew my job was also in jeopardy. If I didn't do what the boss told me to do, I was gone. I also believed that when you make a commitment to somebody, you must give them a chance to fail. It was not only the reasonable thing to do, it was the moral thing to do.

I went into hiding. I avoided meetings. I decided it was a good time to go visit some affiliate stations. I just knew I was going to be fired. It was just a matter of time. Then one day, weeks later, it happened. I was getting out of the elevator. There he was, standing right in front of me, The Boss.

"Frank, have you taken care of that matter we talked about a few weeks ago?"

By now, I had rehearsed this moment of truth a thousand times. I stared back and said, "No, I haven't done a thing."

He looked at me for what seemed to be an eternity, as I died a thousand deaths. Then he smiled and said, "Good, I'm glad. He's really terrific." After I started breathing again, I smiled, too. I was right! People know me as the person who hired Ted Koppel, but I really feel that the moment of truth for me was when I didn't fire him. To this day, I'm glad that I stood up for what I believed, and did the right thing. It also happened to be a very smart thing.

I'm not sure if Ted knew any of this was going on. I'm not even sure how much he knows to this day. Regardless, it was a turning point for me that deepened my confidence in myself and my ability to make good decisions.

Fast Forward a Few Decades

If it were possible for you to call Ted Koppel at Night-Line and say, "Mr. Koppel, 'What is the first thing that comes to your mind when you hear the name "Francis X. Maguire."

He would say, "You're the greatest."

Here's the story, as I recall it. We had a 25-year reunion gathering at Charlie Osgood's house a few years ago for our old ABC Radio Flair Reports Team. It was during the Christmas season. Ted drove up from Washington in his new Mercedes. I imagine he welcomed a trip in his new car on that wintry Sunday afternoon.

It was a warm, wonderful feeling to be with friends whose memories you carried with you all those years. I remember that we were all standing in the living room, playing "Remember the time when" and "Whatever happened to." Ted looked at me and said, "Frank, remember when I was 23, and you put your job on the line and took a chance on hiring me? I will never forget it. I was terrified of failing, and didn't know how long I could hold on.

"But, every single day, you would come by my desk and you'd spend a couple of minutes with me before heading home. You'd ask about my day. You'd acknowledge my good pieces and coach me on those that fell short. And before you left, you'd always look back and say to me, Ted, you're the greatest. And you'd give me that Irish smile and your trademark thumbs up.

"Francis, there were many days when I already had

my piece in the can. I could have gone home, but I didn't. I'd stick around and wait and you'd show up and always give me a shot of self confidence which I really needed and looked forward to at the end of each day. And I want you to know that if I have achieved anything at ABC, a lot of it has to do with the validation you gave me at the age of 23."

That meant so much to me, and I thanked Ted for sharing those recollections. Ted is a dear friend, and if I had anything to do with his magnificent career, I am humbled and grateful. I do remember going out on a limb for him during that time, because I believed in him. He was inexperienced, but had tremendous talent, and I could see it. I could see the light behind his eyes. I made the decision to support him, because it was the right thing to do.

I've never regretted that decision. On the contrary, looking back, I'm glad I chose to stand up for someone I believed in.

I would rather be associated with helping Ted Koppel get started, than remembered as the person who wrote Ted Koppel off as inexperienced and not ready for prime time.

Then came a moment I will never forget.

I had to leave the party early because I was to attend the Christmas reception for the Federal Express employees in the New York City area. I had my coat and scarf on and had just opened the door. The snow was coming down on this cold December evening. Just before I went through the door, I heard Ted's voice.

"Hold it, everyone, Frank's leaving." Everybody looked in my direction and said goodbye. I was trying to make a quiet get-away, but Ted had thwarted it. He walked over to the threshold of the dining room. All eyes shifted to him. With a gentle smile and a glint in his eye, he said, "Frank .... tell me one more time."

It was a magic moment. We looked at each other for

several seconds. Nobody moved or spoke. His face was beaming.

I gave him the thumbs-up and my best Irish smile and said...

Ted, you're the greatest.

I will never forget that moment. In fact, in my heart, I've been back to that gathering many times.

I've had the good fortune to work with some truly great companies. I've learned many things, but the knowledge that continues to burn brightly from my experience is this: Life is not about your job description.

It's not about making the Fortune 500 list.
It's not about turning a profit.
It's not about being Number One.
It is about making a difference.
It is about caring.
It is about building others up.
It is about letting another person know you think they're the greatest.
It is about touching others.
It is about showing character.
It is about people, and . . .
That is leadership.
That is success.
That is our final destination.

Question. When was the last time you validated someone in your life?
An employee?
A child?

A friend?
A mate?
A perfect stranger?

Regardless of your response, one thing I'm sure of is that we need to validate more than we do. We all need to validate more than we do. It's not about motivation. It's about validation. Motivation lasts a very short time. Validation, on the other hand, lasts a lifetime.

People may forget what you say, they may even
forget what you do, but they will never forget how
you made them feel.

When you really care, when you genuinely encourage others, when you let them know you believe in who they are and appreciate what they do, they'll produce beyond your most optimistic expectations.

As for Ted, was it really just a coincidence that he applied for the job? Was it just a coincidence that I was there when Jim Harriott called to ask me to talk to Ted? Was it just a coincidence that there was still one slot available on the roster? Coincidence? . . .Right.

That is why I would suggest that this is also a spiritual journey we are embarking upon. We are attending the Symphony of Life. You must be very careful that when you see the symphony . . . you don't overlook the Conductor.

What pleases me most is the thought that I made a difference in Ted Koppel's life by doing something anybody can do; I validated him, and the rest is history.

YOU'RE THE GREATEST

· CHAPTER TWO ·

WE CARRY OUR TREASURES IN FRAGILE CONTAINERS

"WHAT IS ESSENTIAL IS INVISIBLE TO THE EYE."

My late, dear friend and co-founder of Hearth Communications, John Culkin, used to say, "We carry our treasures in fragile containers." Too often, we are not encouraged to feel good about who we are and what we do. We are not encouraged to feel that despite our mistakes, our physical, emotional or spiritual flaws, there are marvelous treasures inside of us. If we get in touch with those treasures, we can enjoy a very rich and fulfilled life.

Yet, despite our treasures, all of us have this constant gnawing of self doubt. We don't give ourselves the credit that we should, because we were taught as children to be humble, not to be conceited or arrogant. Sadly, at the same time, many of our parents and teachers consistently demanded perfection.

Our exterior layer is very thin. Most of us are more outer than inner directed. Often, someone's lack of a smile, an overlooked comment, or an unresponded to "hello" ruins our day. We are all affected by the actions of others, isn't it logical to assume that you significantly affect the lives of others? It's not whether we affect them, it's how much we affect them. We need to accept and support each other as we are, and let it be okay when someone we lead or love makes a mistake.

Buckminster Fuller put it this way:

> *We are deliberately designed to learn by trial and error. But, we're brought up to think that nobody should make mistakes. Most children get degeniused by the love and fear of their parents . . . that they might make a mistake.*
>
> *But all my advances were made by making mistakes. You uncover what is when you discover what isn't.*

The Home / Work Relationship
Of Your Employees

I think all the time about how little awareness the front-line supervisors and managers have of how significant their thoughts, words, and actions are to their employees. They don't realize that those employees go home and treat their families how they were treated at work by their bosses. These first-level managers have a major role to play in the quality of lives and productivity of their employees.

To fully understand this dynamic, managers need to realize that what happens at work has a direct impact on what happens at home, and what happens at home has a direct impact on what happens at work. In reality, there is no wall between work and home.

We've all known individuals who proclaimed that they "left their work at the office."

Sure they did.

We all have heard that you shouldn't bring your personal life to work with you. Well that may sound good, but it just doesn't work that way. We can't just divide ourselves into segments. We are not personal and professional. We're whole entities. That's what is so unique about being human. Humans have feelings ... we truly carry our treasures in fragile containers.

Leaders must recognize, not ignore, the home/work relationship. They must recognize that an employee is the sum of his or her parts. There is life outside the corporate campus. There are school events, children's birthday parties, aging parents, missed school buses, chicken pox, dance recitals, plumbing emergencies, relationship stress, religious events and don't forget the weekly essentials such as groceries, dry cleaning, meals, and family time.

Effective leaders are able to understand that home and work are infinitely related. They understand that each area impacts the other, and they understand the importance of enhancing the quality of life for their employees, whether they are at home or at work.

There is a clear and definite correlation between how good things are at home and how good things are at work. Happy employees are motivated employees. When you provide an opportunity for a smooth and calm, even uplifting, transition for your employees between work and home, you will get more productivity and return on your investment.

May I Not Be An Obstacle

Productivity is not determined by senior management coming forth with edicts. Employees want to have a positive relationship with their direct supervisor.

Fred Smith, the founder and CEO of Federal Express, created a culture that encouraged managers to make their employees' jobs as easy as possible; To remove any obstacles their employees encountered. Unfortunately, there are other corporations that took a different route, and they are no longer around. Today, managers need to heed the advice of the Latin phrase *Ne Sim Obex*. Translation: May I not be an obstacle.

If you communicate directly or indirectly to your employees that you don't care about them, productivity will drop. They will no longer have the desire to please you or the customer.

However, if you make those employees feel really good about who they are and the job they're doing, productivity begins to increase. They will be more motivated, more enthusiastic and able to perform to higher standards than you ever thought possible. Your employees also have a right to their own personal R.O.I. It is the employees' R.O.I, that drives the company's R.O.I.

This doesn't mean that you turn a blind eye to problems, nor does it mean that you don't have high standards of accountability. Rather, you think in terms of solutions, and that when you expect the best while validating your employees, productivity, and profits can soar.

What it Takes to Make it in Business

In these days of budget cuts, head count reduction and international neck-and-neck competition, the tendency has been to focus on quality and efficiency self-assessments. Quality and efficiency are both necessary in the business place, but if that is your total focus, you're going to miss your target.

Whatever your industry, if you have employees, you're in the people business. You can have the latest computers, the most impressive quality award yet, the newest, cleanest building and even the largest bathrooms, but if you're not focusing on people, your organization is never going to achieve its potential.

I'll grant you that quality is very important in keeping corporate America competitive in the global marketplace. Our quality standards must be not only as high as those of our competitors, but the highest we can possibly make them. Get lazy, and you pay for it. We must continually raise quality, decrease errors, and reduce cycle time. In the race for quality, there is no finish line.

Poor quality is not the root of the problem. As I see it, the issue is far more basic. It begins inside you and inside me. The issue is the heart. The issue is caring. As the wise old fox said to the little Prince, "It is only with the heart that one can see clearly. What is essential is invisible to the eye."

I must first know that we're on the same team. I must then know that you will support me. That you care about me; That you trust me; That you're in my corner; That you see me as more than the deliverer of quality service. Care for each other precedes care for quality. Finishing best is more important than finishing first.

Does that sound a little soft? Let me give you the business rationale. How do you get a motivated work force? More money? Works for a while. Then what? More money? Training? Incentives? Plaques? Threats?

I want you to wake up to the power you have inside you. Don't be afraid to validate. What do I mean by validate? If somebody you believe in tells you that you can do it, chances are, you will. That's validation. We all have experienced days in which somebody gave us a smile, a pat on the back, a high-five, and it completely changed our day. That's validation. Have you ever told your son he did a good job mowing the yard? Have you ever told your daughter how proud you are of her? That's validation.

It's been many years since I occupied the same workplace with Ted Koppel, but he still remembers the way I validated him. Did I praise everything he wrote? No. Did I send pieces back? Yes. Nobody is perfect, but everybody deserves to be validated, even employees who aren't living up to your expectations. Could it be that they just don't have a clear understanding of what you want from them?

When was the last time you validated somebody? Your employees? Your children? Your mate? There's not enough validation going on. Break the trend and you'll set the pace. You will have higher employee satisfaction, attendance, productivity, and retention. Is that reason enough to punch tickets?

Validation is good business.

The only way to have a consistently motivated work force, whether you're there or not, is to communicate that you care. Your employees don't care how much money the company is making, how many national awards the company receives, how to improve quality, reduce cycle time or improve customer service until they know that you care about them. That's the issue. My point? They don't care until you do!

Do employees appreciate the amenities? Absolutely, but they appreciate even more your concern for them. Simply stated, the way you treat them affects your business more than any other variable, and in this labor market, that's a fact you can't afford to forget.

The Pain of Uncertainty

One of the truisms in life is that *the pain of uncertainty is worse than the certainty of pain.* Not knowing can be torture. Have you ever had to wait on lab tests from your doctor? Remember the wait for your college grades to be posted?

Has your spouse ever said, "There's something we really need to talk about, but later, not now." How's that for torture?

Ever had a Monday call from your boss to schedule a Friday afternoon meeting with you but not tell you what it was for? That can produce some stress. Or more often, the four letter F word, F-E-A-R.

You Never Forget Validation

On the other hand, we all have people in our past who have encouraged us: A teacher, a coach, a parent, an uncle, an aunt, a friend or even a passing stranger. You may even remember exactly what they said. Isn't that powerful?

To this day, you probably remember their names. And how they made you feel. I certainly do.

I remember my Aunt Jo who thought I had the greatest sense of humor as a child. Every time I was around her, she would laugh at my stories. I felt like I was really funny. Today, my sense of humor is something I'm noted for. I can tell you that I was a very quiet, reserved, contemplative, child. Aunt Jo allowed me to fly. She validated me, and helped me to unleash my potential.

My mother always praised the good things about me. I had other people who weren't so kind to me. They pushed me to be perfect, but not Mom. My mother is the reason I sing and play the piano today. She told me how much she enjoyed "her son," over and over. She was truly my number one fan. She thought I was the greatest, and told me just that.

Then, there was my English teacher in high school who saw something in me I had not yet discovered. He told me that I would make a good public speaker. His name was Mr. Flood. Years later, after I saw the *Dead Poets Society* with my son, Patrick, we were reflecting on that wonderful movie in which Robin Williams portrayed a teacher who validated his students. Even though he was only 10 at the time, Patrick asked me, "Dad, did you ever have a teacher like that?"

I thought for a second and then the light went on. I said, "I sure did, son. I had two. Mr. Flood and Mr. Caruso." I'll tell you about Mr. Caruso later. As for now, let me tell you about Mr. Flood. I was a fragile young high school freshman, attending a Jesuit military high school. One day I saw my name on the bulletin board as a member of the freshman debating society. Me? No Way!

I panicked and went in search of Mr. Flood, my homeroom teacher. When I found him, I blurted out my discovery, "Somebody made a big mistake in putting me on the bulletin board as a member of the freshman debating society!" Mr. Flood smiled at me and said, "Yes, I know, mister. That was no mistake. I'll see you in the debating hall every Wednesday, at 2:30. Dismissed."

I showed up that first week with my knees knocking and my head pounding and my mouth dry as a bone! Mr. Flood, against all my fears, kept assuring me that I had a gift. He never failed to encourage me. I have often thought, ever since I left Xavier High School, that my livelihood has had something to do with my ability to communicate effectively, which I learned from that early validation.

Mr. Flood's belief in me started me thinking, "Maybe he's right. Maybe I can." As I went through my life as a student, I discovered he was right! He recognized a gift which I had within me, but I did not see.

You and I have the same opportunity. We have the opportunity to recognize the gifts in others, to encourage them to try them on for size, and fly.

By the way, 40 years later, I tracked down Mr. Flood and called to thank him for believing in me when I was so young and fragile. For a few seconds, there was silence on the other end of the phone. Then, a few tears of joy, and I heard the very emotional words, "Thank you, Francis. Thank you." Maybe you need to make a few calls, too. You know, one of the easiest, and most joyful, things you'll ever do is to tell somebody, "Thank you." We never outgrow our need for validation.

Thank you, Mr. Flood.

YOU'RE THE GREATEST

· CHAPTER THREE ·

ABSOLUTELY POSITIVELY
OVERNIGHT

**"CUSTOMER: FROM THE LATIN WORD 'CUSTOM'
A RELATIONSHIP BUILT UPON
FAITH OVER A LONG PERIOD OF TIME."**

I have frequently heard it said that those who ignore history are destined to repeat it. Now, that makes more sense to me than those words of Sachel Page who said, "Don't look back. Someone might be gaining on you." Case in point. With the FedEx case study being taught at business schools around the world, it might seem that the company was absolutely, positively an overnight success. Wrong.

In fact, it was anything but. For those who attend my lectures, I often recall the first night of operations for Federal Express, April 17, 1973. It was quite a night. I'm not sure of the exact number of packages, but it wasn't impressive.

A group of FedEx pioneers, who called themselves the Dirty Thirty, stood at the distribution facility. A 20 foot cargo container with ball bearing wheels was positioned and waiting for the fleet of 23 planes to touch down on the runway and park on the terminal. The moment of truth had arrived. All of those hopes and dreams, the planning and the waiting was about to pay off.

The *Dirty Thirty* ran out and tore open the cargo doors of those 23 planes and unloaded ...16 packages!

That's how it all started. No headlines, no records set, no threat to UPS, Emery, Airborne Express, DHL or Purolator. But that night, at an airport near Memphis, Tennessee, was born a company that would change the way the world does business. Federal Express, the largest venture capital firm ever formed, was to become the first company to ever reach the one billion dollar revenue mark by its 10th year.

You'd have never thought it that night.

Obviously, things got better, but it didn't happen overnight. As a matter of fact, for the first 32 months, we lost approximately a million dollars a month. Vendors threatened us. Pilots had to use their personal credit cards to fill the planes up with fuel, employees worked without wages, and we even asked our employees not to cash their checks if they didn't have to.

Slowly but surely, it began to happen. The hub and spokes idea was working. The business was gradually growing. That was the good news. The bad news? By law, we were using small Falcon aircraft that restricted our lift capacity. We needed more lift, and therefore, larger planes. Unfortunately, because of FAA restriction of 7,000 pounds per aircraft, we faced a very limited future.

Mr. Smith Goes to Washington

Federal Express needed FAA approval to fly larger, heavier planes, like the 727. In the early 1970s, Art Bass, FedEx's president and COO, told me that the FAA had turned down the request Federal Express had made to become exempt from the 7,000 pound lift limit. This was of serious concern. It limited profit and affected the company's ability to compete. We had no where else to turn. The future of the company was in peril.

At the time, I was working as a consultant for Federal Express and would soon translate my consultant status into becoming an employee. In those days, the company didn't even know if it was going to survive. At the time, I was working for the Princeton, New Jersey, consulting firm, Kepner-Tregoe. I was flying from Boston to my home in Nashville, Tennessee. My plane had a short layover in Washington. On an impulse during the twenty minute layover, I grabbed my briefcase and got off the plane.

I took a taxi to the Dirkson Senate Office Building, checked my bag with security, and I walked into Tennessee Senator Howard Baker's office. I put a warm Irish smile on my face and said, "Hi, I'm Frank Maguire, from Memphis.

I'd like to speak to the legislative or administrative assistant for the Senator."

It worked.

The next thing I knew, I was sitting in a small conference room in the outer office with Senator Baker's assistant. I told him that I was there to talk about "my" company in Memphis. How we had the potential for thousands of jobs, and how we were distressed that we were not able to grow any further because of FAA restrictions. I was wondering if he might be able to find a spot on the calendar for Fred Smith and Art Bass to come by and speak to the senator in more detail about it. As luck (and initiative) would have it, I was able to secure an appointment with Senator Baker on the morning of October 24.

I thanked him very much and departed. I walked down the hall and found Senator Bill Brock's office, the other senator from Tennessee, repeated my routine, and Brock's AA scheduled a meeting with Senator Brock in the afternoon of that same day, October 24, neither knowing of the appointment I had made with the other. Since then, I often have wondered if all this was just a coincidence or if there were other forces at work.

Quickly, I found the nearest public phone, called Art Bass and said, "Art, I've set up an appointment for you and Fred with Senator Baker and Senator Brock on October 24. They have agreed to see you to discuss the FAA's decision. Art Bass thanked me. I went back to the airport, and on to my home in Nashville.

Having worked in the executive office of the president (Kennedy and Johnson) for six years, I knew that a regulatory agency was paid billions of dollars to tell you "no." Here was Federal Express, sitting in Memphis, Tennessee, represented by these two and several other powerful sena-tors, such as Mississippi senator Jim Eastland, Missouri senator Fullbright and Arkansas senator John McClellan, the most powerful delegation in the country, all within a stone's throw of Memphis. The senators' willingness to help was re-ally our last card to play.

Art Bass and Fred Smith came to Washington, and were so effective, that Bill Brock and Howard Baker both wanted to claim sponsorship of this young former marine's cause.

At the same time, the airline deregulation bill was mak-ing its way through Congress. Senator Howard Cannon from Nevada, who was managing the bill, was asked by Senators Baker and Brock to have lunch with Fred Smith. Fred so impressed Senator Cannon that after a series of meetings, the senator said, "Mr. Smith, if you will agree to help me by testifying on behalf of this deregulation bill before the Senate Commerce Committee, I will attach an amendment deregulating the freight industry, as well."

The deregulation bill, as proposed, was intended only to deregulate the airline passenger business. Almost every airline fought tenaciously to prevent Federal Express from being included. Fred Smith rose to the challenge, persevered and achieved his mission. He single-handedly convinced Congress to see his vision. Fred Smith was so effective that the day.

President Carter signed the bill into action, I said to myself, "Francis, this could be called the Federal Express Deregulation Bill." In my heart, I smiled, realizing that it all started with a consultant getting off an airplane in Washing-ton, D.C., on the way home from the office.

The important thing for me is not to receive any credit. More importantly, it gave me a sense of accomplishment to know I had a degree of participation in the establishment of Federal Express. Fred's leadership and vision and the hard work of the team around him made it work well, but it wouldn't have left the ground if it weren't for those fateful meetings in Washington.

We all want to be recognized for our participation. I say, give it to them! Share the credit. Share all the credit. It doesn't cost you a thing. There's no limit to what you can accomplish if you don't care who gets the credit.

A Basketball Court of Appeal Versus a Congressional Celebration

There's a postscript to that story. When I worked as the chief personnel officer at FedEx, I used to park my car as far away from the building as I could and then walk through the parking lot so I could meet the hourly employees going to and from the Hub, which is where FedEx packages are received, sorted and shipped. The day President Carter was to sign the bill into law, I met a young man, James, who was the shuttle driver for the flight crews. As I recall, he had the lowest entry pay grade in the company. He approached me in the parking lot, introduced himself, and told me that he had been cut from the basketball team at the Hub. James was very emotional. Despite being a strong defensive player, he didn't score a lot of points. Both of us knew, basketball games are not just won offensively, but defensively, too. Nonetheless, he was off the team.

I told him, "You know, James, I can see you're very passionate about this. Come up to my office and see me. I'd like to talk to you. It's a busy day and I really have to get to my office. But I want to see you. Please come by."

He thanked me and I went up to my office. Since it was the day of the deregulation bill signing, there were television monitors set up around the office, and champagne bottles cooling all over the building. Just as the scheduled was to come before the television cameras, Wanda, my secretary, called from her desk. "Mr. Maguire, there's a gentleman here to see you. James from the HUB."

I told her to send him in. James came in. It wasn't hard to see right away that he was impressed that he was able to get access to a senior officer in the company. My title didn't mean as much to me, but apparently it meant a great deal to him. He came in very reverently and stood there until I invited him to sit down. I walked out from behind my desk and sat down across from him.

He told me the story in more detail of how he was unjustly cut from this basketball team. Obviously, managing one of the company basketball teams was not in my job description, but it meant a lot to James.

As he was telling me his story, I heard the applause outside my office. I heard the champagne bottles popping, and I realized that it was now a done deal; The president had just signed the deregulation bill. I instinctively started to get up from my chair, but inside, from my gut, I heard a voice, *"Francis, stay seated. James is telling you something important. Listen!"*

At that moment I realized that my job was to take care of the needs of the people who worked for the company, Not drink champagne and celebrate a company victory. I could do that in a little while. Right then, my priority was James. I just eased myself back into the chair, and listened. After he shared his story, I told him I would look into the matter and get back to him. He left, very appreciative. He walked through a crowd celebrating the deregulation bill, but he was celebrating the fact that somebody cared enough to listen.

Later that same day, I called the manager of the Hub and asked him to look into James' situation. I found out there were other agendas. There was new management in the Hub who were taking this team very seriously. They placed requirements that you could only play on this team if you were tall and if you were a scorer. James was short and a defensive player, but he was also an employee and a team member. James became a member of the team. He wasn't in the starting lineup, but he was happy. From then on, every time I saw him as he drove past on his bus, he honked the horn and gave me a big high-five.

Later that afternoon, Fred Smith called me to his office and asked me to meet with him as he called the employees to come celebrate at the local watering hole, the Sawmill. That made me feel great.

Around 7 p.m., we walked into the Sawmill after work and there were hundreds of people there. In walked Fred Smith and Maguire. They went crazy. They cut our ties off right underneath the knots and nailed them to the ceiling. It was a true celebration! A real victory party.

It showed me once again that good leadership shares the vision and enthusiasm of the work force. Fred was not the CEO of the company that night. He was the leader. He was the keeper of the dream. The keeper of the vision. He sincerely believed in the company values of People-Service-Profit.

I also learned the irony in the fact that here we were, the overnight team. Yet, we didn't get to this point overnight. It took thousands of people, doing their jobs, day in and day out. That's the only way we could have ever achieved what we did. We took it a day at a time. In bite-size, do-able steps.

Leadership Versus Competency

General H. Norman Schwarzkopf and I speak together from time to time at various conventions. A few years ago, I was with him in Hawaii at a General Motors Convention at the Grand Wailai Hotel. We were housed next door at the Four Seasons. One morning at breakfast, we were talking about his observations of corporate America. "What's missing today in corporate America is *leadership*. And leadership has more to do with character, not competency."

How do you distinguish between leadership and management? Competency is something that can be acquired. It can be learned, it can be bought in a piece of software, but character is what a leader has. *Competency* has to do with management, leadership is a quality of the heart. A leader's character is critical at all times, not just when he or she is in front of the group. This is why the character issue is raised even of political leaders.

It has to do with character. Competency is a subset of leadership. If I had a very competent person with no leadership skills, or a leader with little competency in that field, I'd go with the leader. You can buy competency.

How do you develop character? You *wake up*. Character is awareness. People who have no integrity, number one, don't fool anybody. And, number two, change is from the inside. No one can do it for them. They have to have an inner awakening. They must make a conscious decision to change.

Sit In My Chair

I recall the time when I requested approval for a million dollars for the Federal Express Human Resource Division. We were so committed to our employees, I just anticipated that it would be approved.

I didn't understand why the boss said no. Not only once, but five times. I believed I had always caught him at the wrong time. That's why I persisted.

On Friday afternoon, I walked into Fred's office to wish him a good weekend. "Okay, Fred, I'm out of here," I said.

He looked up and smiled and said, "Okay, Frank. See you Monday. Have a good weekend." He seemed to be in a particularly good mood, so I decided to press my luck one more time. I said, "Have you got a minute?" As I said, I had been trying to gain his approval on this particular project for several weeks. Each time I had presented it, he turned it down. This was the last time, and this time, I was going to succeed.

Fred knew what was coming, and said, "Sure. Do you want to talk about it again?"

I said, "Yeah, just for a few minutes."

He said, "Okay, Frank. Close the door."

So, I closed the door and walked back. Meanwhile, he got up from his chair, the chairman's chair. He said, "Francis, come around to this side of the desk."

I didn't know what was going on, so I walked around his desk. He pulled the chair out and said, "Here, sit down." I hesitated, but he motioned again. So I sat down. He pushed the chair gently to the desk and said, "Now, just lean forward like I do and make your case again."

Then he went around and sat at the chair on the other side of the desk, where I was supposed to be sitting. He looked at me and smiled, and said, "Okay, now tell me. Tell me why I should approve that proposal."

Suddenly I realized that I was looking at my program as the senior personnel officer of the company, and he was looking at it from the viewpoint of the CEO, shareholders, the investment bankers, the operations vice-presidents in the field and all the other staff officers. It was another spin on active listening and understanding, and it was working.

I'll never forget what I said to him next. "Fred, there's only one thing I *really* want."

"What's that?"

I said, "I want to get out of here, right now."

It was a great lesson which continues to educate me to this day and one which I've shared with other heads of corporations. In fact, they wrote the whole story about our Friday meeting in Reader's Digest.

I have now shared the lesson with you, direct from the student's mouth.

Among other lessons I learned, there is no such thing as an overnight success; There is also no such thing as an overnight failure. You and I must be good stewards of our time, our abilities, our resources and our opportunities. That is a never ending process. It also makes each day very exciting because of the potential it holds. That's why I believe that every day tells us that the journey is not over. It has just begun.

YOU'RE THE GREATEST

· CHAPTER FOUR ·

A VALIDATED EMPLOYEE IMPACTS THE BOTTOM LINE

"PEOPLE WHO FEEL GOOD ABOUT THEMSELVES, PRODUCE GOOD RESULTS."

One rainy Friday afternoon, I was working in Washington, DC, at the Commerce Department. President Kennedy's office called asking for a file regarding a meeting that would take place the following week.

On Friday afternoons in Washington, DC, particularly rainy Friday afternoons, everybody wants to do one thing, get home. No one was particularly anxious to leave the Commerce building and navigate traffic to drop something off with a guard at the White House. I was anxious to get involved, so I volunteered.

To my surprise, because it was raining, I was offered a ride in U.S. Ambassador Henry Cabot Lodge's limo. They sent me over in his car. I remember driving through the gate at the White House in the big limousine of the ambassador. Upon arrival, I went into the "fish room" which was the outer room of the president's office.

"Hello," I said, looking for somebody. I wandered in, farther and farther, but there was nobody there. I found the Oval Office. I then got nervous. I found myself at a staircase, and went up to what was the main floor of the public section of the White House. By this time, I was really wondering what was going on. I mean, I went to the White House and nobody was home!

Then, I looked down the hall, and I saw a pair of khaki pants and white shoes. Someone had his legs crossed, and that was all I could see. I walked down the hall, thinking that perhaps this person could take the document off my hands.

I rounded the corner, and there he was, John Fitzgerald Kennedy, sitting on a chair underneath a plaque that said, "Do not sit." He had a legal pad and a pencil. I was stunned. I said, "Excuse me, Mr. President..."

He looked up and said, "Oh no, you're fine." And he smiled.

I said, "I'm Francis Maguire, and I understand you're looking for this file."

He said, "Oh yes. Thank you very much. I appreciate you bringing that over to me."

And, then he said something that I'll never forget. "Can I get you a Coke?" He had a Coke beside him. And I quickly said, "Oh, no sir. That's quite all right."

"Are you sure?" he asked. "I'd be happy to."

And I said, "No, Mr. President, but thank you just the same. Thank you very much. It's an honor to meet you. I really should be going."

"Okay. Thanks a lot, Francis."

I walked down the hall, still trying to regain my equilibrium from my unexpected encounter with the President of the United States. As I walked down the hall, I turned around before I went back down the stairs, and I saw the president, sitting in the same position, writing. It occurred to me that I should have stayed, and had a Coke. I believe the president was lonely, and he was looking for some company. And for some reason, at that moment, there wasn't anybody else around, and he asked me to share a Coke with him. On a rainy afternoon in Washington, in the very early 60s, I missed an opportunity to have a Coke with a guy by the name of John Kennedy. I regret to this day that I didn't stay.

We carry our treasures in fragile containers. It doesn't matter what your position says on your business card. We all need other people. I would also say, we owe it to each other to recognize the opportunities to validate each other in large and small ways. Stay vigilant for those times. It could be a cup of coffee with a friend, throwing the ball around with your son, sharing the sunset with your spouse or significant other, or having a Coke with the President. In each case, no matter how large or how small, a missed opportunity is a missed opportunity.

Not Luggage But Baggage

It is inherent in human nature for everyone of us to find the good and praise it, to understand a need and fill it, and   see an opportunity to validate and do it!

Good job!
Well done!
I'd be happy to make that call for you.
Have a great trip!
You don't have to go through this alone.
I'll handle it.
How can I help?
Are you ok?

People in the hospitality business think that how you handle the luggage is important. We're all in the hospitality business, and the issue is not the luggage, but the baggage, personal baggage.

We need to be aware, and wake up to what this is about. It's not about a person's title or money. It's about seizing the opportunity to support each other; To let them know they're needed, wanted, and appreciated. That frees them up to produce.

As employers, we need to validate our employees if we want them to grow and operate at their very best. As parents, we need to validate our children if we want them to be fulfilled and independent. As husbands and wives, we need to validate our mates if we want them to be grateful for our being in their lives. As companions, we need to validate our friends so they can know how much we care about them.

I know many very wealthy people with impressive titles who also have very fragile containers. Regardless of how things appear on the surface, you never know what's in the heart.

If we really knew why people do what they do to us, we would forgive them. That all ties back to the issue of validation. With the next era of the global economy, where competitors are coming from all over and technology is threatening on every front to replace people, the concept of validation in the corporate culture becomes a life ring. Those companies who recognize it and can make the transition are going to be:

1) more efficient
2) more productive
3) more responsive
4) much more profitable

Let us not forget: Validation equals earnings. No piece of technology is going to sustain earnings for a corporation without a passionate, committed human being. One important way you get people to feel passionate about their jobs is to make them feel good about who they are. In a word, validation.

A Trip to the White House

While working at the Executive Office of the White House, I was invited to join a group of reporters at the National Press Club to have an off-the-record roast in the restaurant of the National Press Club, just a few blocks from the White House. No invitations were sent. It was just an informal gathering. We were having a meal together, and the roast was underway. It was hysterical. All kinds of outrageous things were said. All of a sudden, the elevator door opens, and out of the elevator steps the President!

We all were stunned. We didn't know what to do, first of all because here was the president, and secondly, because he was the subject of many of the jokes. He smiled, found a seat, and said, "Don't let me interrupt you." He told us to continue, and so, we did. He sat there as a member of the audience, as we continued our roast.

Somehow, he had learned about this little get-together, an occasion to have some fun at his expense. He managed to sneak out of the White House and find our gathering. He had a great time. The President ended up staying for the whole thing. As a matter of fact, many of us walked him back to the White House. It was quite amusing to walk down Pennsylvania Avenue, up to the gate of the White House with the president.

The guards were surprised, and security appeared from everywhere. What a night that was. Once again makes the point that regardless of your station in life, we all need to reach out to each other. I love the song sung by Big Mama Thornton, the great blues singer. She sang the song with such passion. The words, as I remember, go something like this:

I asked my man for a nickel,
and he gave me a 20 dollar bill.
I asked him for a sip of whisky,
and he went out and bought me a whisky still.

Take time to laugh at yourself. You'll feel a lot better. You really are special, and, like everyone else, far from perfect. Celebrate your imperfections. Laugh at yourself.

Perception Is and Can Change Reality

Sometimes, the way you feel is more important than reality. Are you going to make mistakes? Yes. Will you bat

1,000? No. How do you bridge the gap between feelings and reality?

With leaders. A work force is defined by its leaders. Leaders must believe in their employees. If leaders make employees feel like they are *capable* of achieving a goal, they will. If leaders communicate to employees that they believe in them, they will believe in themselves. If leaders think employees are the greatest, employees will think that about themselves. Individuals can achieve anything , if someone they respect believes that they can.

That's exciting news! Belief in ourselves and others can be a jump start for real change. All of a sudden, familiar clichés start having a little more reality:

> *They can who believe they can.*
> *If you can dream it, you can achieve it.*
> *Inch by inch, anything's a cinch.*
> *You'll see it when you believe it.*
> *You become what you think about.*
> *If you think you can or you can't, either way, you're right.*
> *The best way to predict the future is to invent it.*
> *Life is a self-fulfilling prophecy.*

When you begin letting others know they really are capable of achieving great things, they actually begin achieving great things. I've seen it happen first hand in half a dozen corporate cultures.

I know of a group of employees who worked for several years with little or no significant increase in revenue. Then a new leader came in. He let the employees know that he cared about them and they believed in him. The workplace became more enjoyable and everyone shared his vision and his concerns.

All of a sudden, things started changing: Absenteeism went down, turnover reduced, morale went up. Productivity went up, new accounts came in, old accounts started ordering more, and employee and customer complaints went down.

Now, here's the question. What had changed?
The intelligence level of the employees?
The skill level of the employees?

No. Same employees. Same intelligence. Same skill level. What had happened was a change in leadership. These employees began to see themselves differently. They saw the future differently.

Perception changes reality.

You can see it when "leaders" take the helm of a corporation, and sometimes after they leave. Look at Eastern Airlines, before and after Eddie Rickenbacker, the founder and visionary. When you replace leaders who know and appreciate the needs of their customers with number crunchers and bean counters, start watching the newspaper every day because the obituary is coming.

Did the company have the technology? Yes. Did the company have the financial support? Yes. What happened? They lost focus on what was the essential ingredient for a successful company. They were in the people business, and forgot.

Shareholders would be better served if the corporate leaders treated their employees better, who in turn will treat their customers better, who, in turn, will keep doing business with you. That will remain a reality.

Take Away the Obstacles in Leadership

As I have suggested, you can no longer rule by edict. Today, you must lead by persuasion, by example, and by validation. Whatever your level of management, your leadership has a profound impact. You need to be conscious of that. Send your employees home each night, feeling good, not bad, about themselves.

At FedEx, Fred Smith created a culture that encouraged its management team to make their employees' jobs as easy as they could be made. To remove the obstacles. Other organizations have exactly the opposite philosophy. They think the quickest way to the bottom line is to slash operating expenses, regardless of who gets hurt in the process.

When you understand the difference between the two ideologies, employee validation always wins. One grows productivity. One kills it. One makes money. One saps the vitality of the organization.

Did you know that most heart attacks occur at the business place on a Monday morning? Why? A fear-based work place is incredibly stress producing. And who hasn't had that gut-wrenching fear of the boss asking to see you on Friday afternoon? How does it make you feel? In many companies, you might as well start cleaning out your desk, because you are about to be fired.

To create and sustain a motivated work force, you must be able to remove the stress and fear. Both take way too much energy. An employee can't concentrate on productivity or creativity if he or she is worried about keeping their job. When you remove those barriers, employees begin to soar!

Here's a maxim for you as a leader: The main thing is to keep the main thing, the main thing. What are your main things? Employees, customers, validation, clear communication, concern, productivity, creativity, and profit.

If you can keep your focus, you will succeed. But keep your focus. It's up to you. Believing is seeing the ability of your employees to reach corporate goals. Believing is becoming the organization you want to become. That kind of employee validation transforms reality into dollars and *sense*.

There are two things that will never happen again – today, and you.

YOU'RE THE GREATEST

· CHAPTER FIVE ·

EFFECTIVE LEADERSHIP
COMMUNICATION

**"WHO YOU ARE IS SPEAKING SO LOUDLY,
I CAN'T HEAR WHAT YOU'RE SAYING."**
Ralph Waldo Emerson

People who feel good about themselves do indeed produce good results. Sometimes it happens right under your nose. If you watch and observe carefully, you'll see what I mean.

I was present the night that a young and untried TV host did his very first interview show on television. It was in New York City. The year was 1952. I was a freshman at Fordham University, working my way through college. He walked into the newsroom at WABD, Channel 5, the flagship of the old DuMont Television Network. I was the associate producer for the 11 p.m. news. The ratings at Channel 5 were so bad that they jettisoned the 11 o'clock news and replaced it with a new format. It was an interview format called *Nightbeat*.

We were very nervous, wondering what we were going to do this first night without the usual 11 o'clock news. Wondering, perhaps, if there would be a second night. Down the hall came the producer, Ted Yates. He introduced himself and explained, "This is a pilot program that we're putting together. A work in progress. It's going to be an interview format with a different approach." He didn't describe it any further. Then a second gentleman walked into the room. "This is my associate, Mike Wallace," Ted said.

"Nice to know you, Mr. Wallace," I said.

It was about to hit the fan!

That night, when we went on the air, Mike Wallace interviewed a well-known union leader who was known for his questionable practices, and Wallace took him to the woodshed! The subject was the subway employees' union. Mike was interviewing the head of the union. The union was threatening to strike and shut down the subway, which, in turn, would shut down New York City.

The union head didn't know this young interviewer. But he always looked for opportunities to be on television and advance his cause. He accepted the invitation, planning to intimidate and dominate Wallace, just like he did everyone else. Once the program started, Wallace practiced his craft, with his wry look, and kept his barrage of questions coming. The union leader unraveled. He called Wallace a scalawag. There was a moment when he came very close to storming off the set. I sat in the control booth with my mouth wide open. This was fun. It was different. Wallace was on his way.

Back in the early 50s, this was not the way personalities were treated on television. But Wallace invented himself on television that night. Move over Steve Alien! It became the number one night-time show in New York City. This was just the beginning.

Years later, Dick Cavett, Mike Wallace and I were having a lunch over at the Des Artistes, which was the hangout for many of us at ABC. At the time, Cavett hosted a late-night show opposite *The Tonight Show*. Cavett was different. He had an intellectual style of interviewing. Wallace was a Cavett fan, too. Dick said something to Mike which has stayed with me to this day, and it really captures what I'm trying to get across to leadership teams that I talk to and train. The issue is self-confidence.

Cavett said to Wallace, "Mike, from the very beginning, everything you have touched in this industry has turned to gold. You have been a street reporter and it's great. You have been a television interviewer and it took the ratings by storm. You are now a nationally known reporter on 60 Minutes. What is there about you that makes everything work?"

I wondered that same thing. What was it about Mike Wallace? What was it about Henry Ford? What was it about Fred Smith? What was it about Jack Welch? What was it about Jack Kennedy? What was it about Bill Gates? What is it about these people that makes them so successful?

There's got to be a quality that's within them that they share in common.

Mike Wallace answered the question for me.

He looked Cavett in the eye with all the intensity he is so well-known for, and he said, "Well, Dick, I'll tell you, ever since childhood, I've always known how to take the stage."

How to take the stage! Enter self-confidence. The ability to project your inner faith in yourself! Before Mike Wallace even thought about broadcasting as a profession, he already knew how to take the stage.

Each of the leaders I just mentioned knew how to take the stage. They had total self-confidence with grace and dignity. Shakespeare told us, *'life is a stage'*, and how we take that stage will determine how far we go in life, how far we rise in the corporate world, how far we go in the relationships we have in the community, and how effective a parent we are. Life is a series of stage entries.

That's why people who aspire to leadership positions must consider this question: How do you take the stage? When you're making a presentation, when you're making a sales pitch, when you're delivering legislation, when you're rendering an opinion, how do you take the stage?

It's not only your content-what you say-but how you take the stage. I spend quite of bit of my time speaking to large audiences. I think leaders spend too much time preparing with their head and not nearly enough with their heart.

Whether it's in front of a small or a large group of employees or customers, you have to communicate with your heart as much as, if not more than, with your head. The heart is what touches others. It's what motivates others. It allows others to see and respond to who you are and what you feel. It helps them sense your passion, and that creates loyalty..

People will forget what you do.
People will forget what you say.
They will never forget how you made them feel.

As a leader, you must speak from the heart if you want a dedicated, motivated, loyal work force. If you lead from the heart as you validate others, you're going to succeed.

People love to follow leaders who know how to take the stage, and while you're up there, make them feel they're the greatest. That's a key that's easy to forget. The stage is not about the spotlight shining on you. It's about turning the spotlight on others! In so doing, you share the stage. You do that with words, actions, and with your entire demeanor. In short, use every vehicle from your public position to applaud and support others.

What's Up There on Stage With You?

That leads to your non-verbal skills. If John Kennedy, at his inaugural address, had simply stood in front of that massive audience in 1960 and read from a piece of paper, "Ask not, my fellow Americans, what your country can do for you. Ask, rather, what you can do for your country," that statement would not have become so famous. Those of us who were there, who remember it well, remember that finger pointing at the audience, and that Irish smile, and that passion in his voice.

I'll tell you Jack Kennedy's gift: He knew how to take the stage, and he knew how to speak from the heart. Most of the leaders that I have known in my life who would be considered to have achieved success, have also been people who knew how to take the stage and speak from the heart.

Not everyone knows how to take the stage with dignity and grace. But the fact is that we ALL take the stage.

You must be aware of that. You are on the stage, my friend. I think the difference between success and failure in many facets of our lives is that some of us forget that we are on the stage. You may not realize it, but you're still there. It's a metaphor. And we're all members of the cast.

I want to help raise your level of awareness. You know, when I say to audiences all over the world, "You need to validate instead of motivate," no one disagrees. Then why don't we do it? Because we are asleep. We are not as aware of it as we should be.

In what ways do you take the stage each and every day? You do it by your actions. You do it by your words. You do it with your heart. You do it by your silence. You do it by your thoughts, your gestures and your attitudes. The issue is this: You may not always do it well, but you always do it. You cannot not be on stage - Dad, Mom, manager, coach, boss, husband, wife, son, daughter, Granddad, Grandmother. You cannot not communicate. The people who count are watching you, and you have an opportunity to have a profound and lasting effect on them.

You might as well admit it; Others notice your actions and your reactions. They notice how you act when you're angry, how you react when you're cut off in traffic, or what you do when you've made a mistake.

More importantly, they know if you're speaking from the heart, and whether your heart is in your work. Not only do people know what you think about them, they can also feel your passion or lack of it.

I am trying to take a mirror, put it close to your face, and say, "Look!" My goal is for you to know that and begin acting like you're on stage. Act in such a way that it's okay for others to see who you are and how you act. If you're not okay with that, then I suggest to you, that's a warning sign. Change whatever you need to change, because whether you like or not, there you are, up on stage. The curtain is up and the lights are on. It's showtime!

Whether or not there's anybody in the theater, the curtain is going up. The issue is how you take the stage, even when there's nobody in the theater but you.

The Stage is Not Always a Popular Place to Be

Wayne Hizenger, the founder and CEO of Autonation, took the stage at a recent JD Power annual round table meeting in San Francisco, which preceded the National Automobile Dealers Association (NADA) meeting. The dealers were there to see the enemy. They were angry with him and nervous and anxious over what he was doing to their industry. They were also curious about what he might say to them from the stage.

Let me tell you how Wayne Hizenger took the stage. He acknowledged to me beforehand that he was nervous, but that he couldn't pass up this opportunity. He stood up in front of the convention of automobile dealers, some of whom were billionaires, and he said, 'I'm here to talk to you about what we are doing at Autonation. Your industry as we know it traditionally spends most of its time and attention and millions of dollars on how to sell cars — the selling experience. Autonation has been looking at the buying experience. What does the buyer want and expect?

'We have identified with the buyer, and you're thinking, 'How can I sell?

'This is the industry that gave away the oil change and lube business, and the tire business. If you buy a car from a company, where would be the natural place for you to go to get a tire? The same place you bought the car. But you gave that away.'

Hizenger knew that everybody in that room wanted a piece of him. He knew that he was not the most popular person in the room. But he also knew that how he took the stage — confident, positive, accurate, humorous, with a smile — underpinned the message: It's the buyer's experience that you need to focus on, and he spoke from the heart.

That day, I saw men of substance shake their heads as he was talking and say, "This man is telling us something we know. Why have we not been aware of it?"

Wayne Hizenger was there not to gain monetarily. He was there to say, "Look, I'm not the bad guy. We're just doing the obvious."

He didn't come in with a secret formula, but he drove his message home by taking the stage. By challenging the audience with a different perspective, he gained the team's respect and they began to believe in his message. He was a smash.

Take the Stage With a Clear Message

Federal Express: The largest venture capital firm ever formed, in a crowded and very competitive arena, an enterprise that lost a million dollars a month for 32 months. Now that's taking the stage. Yet from day one, Fred Smith, the founder, had two solid corporate objectives:

> *Objective Number 1:* 100% customer satisfaction
> after every transaction
> *Objective Number 2:* 100% commitment to
> service from every employee

Fred Smith and Federal Express took the stage and dramatically got that message out there. Not just with words, but with actions and professional couriers who knew what they were doing and looked the part, with bright and boldly colored aircraft you could literally see in the sky. With dramatic delivery deadlines they met. Did you ever have any doubt about what the message was? When you think of the words, "Absolutely, positively, overnight," who comes to mind immediately? When it absolutely, positively had to be there overnight, who did you think of?

These young men and women not only took the stage, they made their company name a verb. FedEx.

That's taking the stage.

That's sharing a vision with your employees.

That's having a passion.

That's communicating from the heart.

That's having a very ambitious goal and believing that your work force can pull it off.

They knew from day one that they were the greatest. Several years later, everyone agreed. But FedEx knew it from the start.

YOU'RE THE GREATEST

· CHAPTER SIX ·

CORPORATE AMERICA'S COMMUNICATION PROBLEM

"YOU CANNOT NOT COMMUNICATE."

I really believe that corporate America has a major communications problem. The root cause of that problem is the need for a corporate culture based upon three steadfast commitments:

- Share the vision
- Share the information
- Share the responsibility

Share the Vision

Share where you want to go. Share your dreams. You don't think your employees want to know? Ask them! They'll help you get there. As many leaders will tell you, when you leave employees in the dark, they will fill in the blanks, and usually they're wrong. You can prevent this by regularly sharing your dreams and plans for the future with them. Here's where we are today, and here's where we're going, here's how we're going to get there, and here's how you can help.

We need to share the dream, the vision, with our employees. What is the vision of your enterprise? What do you want to accomplish? Fred Smith didn't deliver packages and Colonel Sanders didn't make the gravy. They dreamed and shared the vision of what they wanted their companies to become.

JFK shared his vision of a future America, and changed the way the world looked at our nation. You will find that when true leaders arrive, they come with a vision. Jack Welch's vision for General Electric took it from a 14-billion dollar company in the early 80s to an over 500-billion dollar company today. Someone once asked Dwight Eisenhower what was the most important element needed in winning wars. General Eisenhower said, "The most important thing in winning a war is morale." He didn't say bullets, bombs, battleships. He said morale. Morale is tied to looking ahead, and feeling good about the future.

You have to give people a dream to share with you. Walt Disney had a dream and he shared it with his employees. Henry Ford had a dream and he shared it with his employees. People need to catch the dream, in order for them to feel emotionally involved and committed.

They're asking, "Why are we here? What are we doing? What's the purpose of our coming together?" When they share your dream, people will strive to do what you need done. Whatever it takes to keep the dream alive and well and growing.

The risk you take in sharing your dreams is that not all of them will come true. Yet, I think your employees will understand. They will appreciate that you care enough about them to share your dreams with them, and they will work even harder to help turn your dreams into a reality.

Of course, before you can have a dream come true, you must *first* have a dream. I submit that dreams energize employees. Your company needs a dream. If you don't have one, that should be a high priority for you right away. Visualize your dream, put words around it, then share it.

This is not only true for CEOs, but also for all leaders. Share your dreams with your employees, friends, kids, and partners. Keep the dream alive.

Share the Information

The people who work in your organization are going to go home tonight and watch CNN or one of the other cable networks; they're going to read *USA Today* or the local paper. They're going to be up on what's happening *all over the world* . . . and yet, they're probably not going to know a thing about what's happening at the heart of their company. In this information rich society that we live in, where people can get on the internet and find out anything they want to know about any subject, it just isn't acceptable for them to put their head on the pillow at night, not knowing what's going on at work. Remember, the pain of uncertainty is much worse than the certainty of pain.

What does that communicate? How can you change it? You must share information. In my experience, there is seldom a downside to employees having access to information. On the contrary, if you don't supply it for them, they will learn about it one way or another. Or, worse, they will make something up. If your employees aren't getting reliable information from you, your relationship with them will suffer, as will the company.

People want to know. Good news or bad, they want to know. If money is tight, they want to know. If competition is strong, let them know. If the shareholders are raising concerns, tell them. If a performance appraisal is less than acceptable, share the information. Most people will tell you, "I only wish I had been told."

I wish I had a nickel for every time the only thing standing between me and successfully accomplishing my task was my boss. He had vital information that he didn't share with me. Your employees can't act on information they don't have. They will feel they are building a bridge to nowhere, rather than connecting with opportunities which are now here.

You can track a successful company by how effectively it communicates with its employees. Then, their employees communicate with the customer. If employees are fully informed they are not preoccupied with the problems of the organization. That frees them up to concentrate on the customer.

Dr. W. Edwards Deming, a pioneer in the international quality movement, did some research in this area and found that 90 percent of productivity problems in corporate America are management-related. In short, they didn't ask the employees before putting a plan in action, nor did they inform the employees of the corporate plan.

I remember when we first began putting our couriers in uniforms at Federal Express. The manager in charge of the project had the uniform designed and was ready to have it manufactured. When she asked me to sign off on the final stage, I asked what the couriers thought of the design. The response was, "They're going to love it."

I asked, "Do you mean they haven't seen them yet?"

"Of course not."

I knew the adverse consequences of this decision. We were about to sign a check for a few million dollars, and the potential was that the couriers would not even like them. We quickly put together a group of couriers from the field, representing all regions of the country. We brought in designers and some models with the new proposed uniforms.

Five minutes into the meeting, we discovered that the original design would have been a disaster because it overlooked some important aspects of life out on the road. The employees helped design a highly functional, durable, and attractive uniform which won the immediate approval of our courier force, and was the envy of, and the model for, the industry. The employees felt great. It not only makes good people sense to share your vision, it also makes very sound financial and management sense, too!

By trying to hide information, the leaders only make things worse. Your employees can handle bad news. They understand critical, uncertain circumstances. Above all, they can rise to the occasion. They will surprise you by their loyalty and dedication. First, you have to share information and take them into your confidence.

Share the Responsibility

There's a saying the Bank of America uses: *Ne Sim Obex.*Translation: *May I not be an obstacle.* Leaders, get out of the way. Don't be an obstacle. We spend millions of dollars to recruit and train new employees, and then we get in their way and don't let them do their job; We micro-manage. Employees often don't do their job because they don't have a sense of the vision, they don't have the information they need, and they don't feel validated and appreciated.

Instead we have a sales contest, a quality contest or a productivity contest, and for this month, people will be running around, looking for a bonus check or a trip. I want a company that enables leaders to leave. Leaders who validate their employees by allowing them to do their job, without interference.

Give your employees the opportunity to fail. They are going to disappoint you. Because we don't share the responsibility, we often only give people the chance to fail, not succeed. We interfere. As a result, the employees have been conditioned to do nothing in the event of crisis but wait for the boss. They know management will take care of it. It's like a spoiled child who has learned to respond, "Everything will be okay. Dad will give me the money." That's no way to grow a family or a company.

As a leader, you don't have to shoulder the burden of responsibility alone. Share it. Share the work and share the responsibility. It's called delegation, and you have to do it.

You have a choice. You can choose to micro-manage and stick your nose into as many nooks and crannies of your business as possible. Or you can trust your people to successfully handle what you hired them to do.

Employees soon catch on. Why even try to figure out the job when the boss will just undermine their work? This learned lethargy and inertia can be lethal to your company's well-being. Besides, who are you trying to protect? You do your employees a deep disservice when you withhold responsibilities from them.

Share the vision, *share* the information, and *share* the responsibility. That puts many more oars in the water.

YOU'RE THE GREATEST

· CHAPTER SEVEN ·

THE FOUR LETTER "F" WORD

"FEAR."

The night before my quadruple by-pass surgery, I was unaware that my daughter, Elisabeth, was in my darkened hospital room. When I moved my leg, I heard her say, "Are you okay, Dad?" I didn't know she was in the room. But there she was, all knotted up in that plastic chair in the corner.

"Sure, Libby. I'm fine!"

"Are you scared, Dad?" she asked in her quiet voice.

And I said, "Yeah, Libby. I'm scared to death."

There was a brief pause, and my daughter said to me, in that dark hospital room, "It's okay, Dad. It's okay to be scared."

I'll never forget that night or the impact my daughter's words had on me. You bet I was scared, scared to death. And my teenage daughter slayed my dragon of fear by telling me it was okay to be scared. She validated my feelings. I did not have to be strong. I did not have to put up a facade. It was okay with her, and okay for me to share my fear.

What a life-changing lesson that has been for me. It is okay to be scared. I don't have to be Superman anymore. Only when I share those fears and anxieties with others, can they help me carry the load. Sharing those fears is also a part of sharing the responsibility.

We need to learn to validate people in every way, which includes assuring them that it's okay to be scared. Let's face it. We can't see around the bend in the road. Life is quite a journey.

We would be very surprised if we knew just how many of the same insecurities, the same doubts, the same hang ups, the same limitations, the same fears we all share. It might also be very comforting and reassuring. It still amazes me that when I open up, when I say to audiences, "I'm really afraid of . . ." and I fill in fill in the blank, they nod their heads and respond by saying, "I know. I feel the same way."

We all have fears. Our responsibility to ourselves and to others is first to be aware of them and make an act of faith in ourselves and in others to watch them diminish. All fears: Fear of being fired, fear of downsizing, fear of failure, or fear of success.

An effective leader must know what those fears are and be able to communicate compassion, concern and openness in the face of those fears. Difficult things do happen. There's just no denying it. A leader also must be effective in facing fear, in communicating how to face fear, and in preventing fear from paralyzing the work force.

To a leader, the four-letter 'F' word is FEAR. President Roosevelt didn't say, "One of the things." He said the "only thing we have to fear is fear itself." Fear is what cracks our containers. Leaders remove the element of fear, or uncertainty. What do most people fear? The unknown. A leader can help remove that fear by showing employees that they can help invent their own future.

Achieving and sharing a vision involves risk. That involves fear. Our ability as leaders to identify and effectively combat fear is essential to reaching corporate goals. We must acknowledge and keep fear in check. Not ignore it.

A real leader keeps that vision alive by communicating in such a way that employees want to follow. A manager is someone who runs a step behind you and kicks you on the backside, shouting, "Move out." A leader is the one who runs ahead of you, looks over his shoulder and says, "Come on, we can make it, we're going to get there! Follow me."

A Pledge for a Lifetime

Often times, people come up to me and say, "Frank, you're right on the money. My boss doesn't communicate. Why?" I have a somewhat biased answer.

First of all, let me give you my definition of communication. Communication is *message sent*, *message received*, *message responded* to. Let me tell you a little story. Come with me to 4512 193rd Street in New York City.

As a nine-year old youngster in New York, I loved to listen on my secreted, one-tube radio set, with the earphone under my pillow, to the Dodger baseball games. All of New York City not only listened but came to a dead stop when the Dodgers and the Giants played. This was one of those games. I remember it well.

It was a benefit game for Cerebral Palsy. Red Barber came on the radio, "Call Murray Hill 7-7777 and make a pledge and we'll send you an autographed picture of the Dodgers or the Giants. I'm listening to the game and hearing this number, Murray Hill 7-7777, and his plea. Being a New York kid, you know how much I wanted that picture. I really did. There was no way I was going to miss this chance. "Murray Hill 7-7777," Mr. Barber said.

Finally, it was the ninth inning, I sneaked out of bed and looked downstairs to make sure my parents were still down in the living room with their company. I tiptoed into their bedroom and picked up the phone. The operator asked for the number. I said, "Murray Hill 7-7777".

"Dodger Baseball," the volunteer operator said. "What is your name please?"

"F-F-Francis M-Maguire."

"What is your address?"

"4512 193rd Street."

"Would you like to make a pledge?"

Silence.

I took a deep breath.

Here I go!

"I pledge allegiance to the flag of the United States of America. . ."

I go through the entire pledge, slam the phone down, run down the hall and slide into bed . . . safe. My heart was pounding. Three days later, when I came home from school, my grandmother said, "Francis, you've got something in the mail."

I can see it to this day. It was a tube. I opened it and pulled out . . . both autographed team pictures. The Dodgers and the Giants. I've thought often about that lady who sent me both pictures because she picked up on what had happened, and she rewarded me because I had courage to make that call.

What the word *pledge* meant to me was not what it meant to her. As I said, I define communications rather simply: Message sent, message received, message responded to. You have to look at all three, because all three are important.

> *Message sent:* It needs to be clear.
>
> Message received: It needs to be understood and acknowledged.
>
> *Message responded to:* This measures the effectiveness of your communication.

We don't have a problem with ways to send or receive messages. Telephone, fax, email, pagers, even letters and memos. And then there's my favorite: between four eyes.

Message sent, not a problem. Message received, not a problem. But here's the problem: message responded to. We somehow feel that sending and receiving the message constitutes the end of the equation. It doesn't. It's just the beginning.

What does that mean? It's not the technology you use. Face-to-face communication is always the best. The fact is that people like to work for and do business with people they like. Your customers and your employees will vote with their feet if you show them an attitude of indifference. If you drop the ball, admit it. That's one thing. If you appear indifferent, the game is over.

As a matter of fact, research has proven that around 90 percent of the customers you lose, leave not because of being mad, but because they feel you are indifferent toward them. What kind of a message is that? You can have every kind of technology available to allow you to send a message to your customers or employees, but if they think you're indifferent toward them, they're gone. An attitude of indifference communicates powerfully. Make sure you know what message being received by your employees and your customers.

You can't be sure, just by words, that you've sent the right message.

Here's an epilogue to my story. I've had the privilege of knowing personally some of the world's top business and national leaders. People who shaped the course of world events. Yet, I have just recounted for you an episode from my life which profoundly touched me and one that I remember vividly to this day. I do not know the name of the lady who took my pledge nor do I know how old she was. I know nothing about her. Except . . .

That lady who happened to answer the phone responded to that young boy by sending both photos. She probably forgot about my pledge within the year. Maybe before she got off work that night. I have remembered that gesture for a lifetime.

Along the way to our dreams and goals, we have opportunities every day to validate others. I made a pledge that night, and I was fortunate enough to have an angel on the other end of the phone. I'd like to suggest that you join me in making a different kind of pledge today; To be an angel for someone else. Message sent. . . Message received. . . Message responded to.

This gift of responsiveness manifests itself in many different forms, depending upon the opportunity:

> To serve as a reference for someone looking for a job.
> To send a thank you card.
> To return a phone call.
> To give a compliment.
> To be a little more patient.
> To show a little compassion.
> To listen.
> To make someone feel better.

Will this habit make you any more money? Probably not. Further your career? Not likely. Is there anything in it for you. No. Will it require extra energy? Some. Yet today, tomorrow and every day, we have that same opportunity as my unknown angel did 60 years ago. I have thanked her many times by passing along to others this kindness she showed to me.

Even when you are not being kind to others for the sake of making more money, in the end, it will cause you to make more money! It's a lifestyle of genuine unselfish behavior that will generate loyalty in employees and customers. I would hasten to encourage you to be kind to others just because it's the right thing to do, whether it ever put an extra nickel in your pocket, and a lot more enjoyable too!

As my dear friend in Atlanta, Tom Lewis, said to me not long ago, *"Sooner or later, everyone of us will sit down to the banquet table of consequences."* Let every day be a banquet.

The Importance of Non-Verbal Communication

Most of us make the mistake of equating communication with words. Words certainly are important, but I consider the critical piece of communication to be non-verbal. Why? Because that's where we get our power and opportunity to validate. That's the kind of communication we need to send and receive every day. It makes or breaks your efforts at validation.

What are some non-verbal tools to make us more effective communicators ?

First, *facial expressions*. Ever come home from work and have the kids say, "Mom, don't go near Dad."

"Why? What did he say?"

"Nothing. You should see his face." Careful.

Have you ever made a presentation and you knew from your client's facial expression how it was being received?

Ever given a talk to your employees and saw from their faces what they thought about what you were saying? It's not hard to see if they agreed or disagreed, if they were bored, if they were ready to leave, or if they were right there with you, really into what you were saying.

Then there's your *tone of voice*. A person's tone is often more important than what he or she is actually saying. Is he saying it through gritted teeth? Is she saying it with a smile? Is it with enthusiasm? Is it lifeless? Is it a growl? Your tone of voice is the lubricant that helps the pill go down.

Next, *Body Language*. It's easy to see just in the way a person shakes your hand if they're glad to meet you, isn't it? Do they look you in the eye? Do they grab your hand firmly? It's not hard to know if someone is glad to see you, and we deduce this without them ever saying a word.

Have you ever been in a room and noticed when

someone looks at their watch? We all have. If I'm speaking to an audience of hundreds of people, and you look at your watch, chances are I'll see you. It's a major indicator that you are ready for me to quit.

Say, "You're the greatest," in a flat tone, with no sincerity while I'm looking for my keys, my voice is saying one thing, but the rest of me is saying something else. But, if I say, "You're the greatest!" with enthusiasm in my voice, as I look you in the eye, smile, and shake your hand, you sense I really mean what I say.

If you meet with an employee and sit with your arms crossed, you deliver a message. Even if you say nothing, you deliver a message. If you avoid eye contact, you deliver a message. Remember, you cannot not communicate.

Non-verbal communication is the catalyst that supports or dilutes your words. It pegs you as an advocate or an adversary, as sincere or hypocritical. Your non-verbal communication can successfully get you to the other side or leave you standing on the wrong side of the river. They are much louder than the words you say.

If people have to choose, they'll always trust the actions over words, because actions rarely lie. Make sure your words match your actions and your actions match your words. Only then, will you get the response you seek.

YOU'RE THE GREATEST

· CHAPTER EIGHT ·

DON'T MESS WITH THE GRAVY

"THE DEVIL'S IN THE DETAILS."

In 1969, the Kentucky Fried Chicken Corporation was the fastest growing company on the New York Stock Exchange. Acquired a few years earlier by John Brown and Jack Massey, the company was taken public. It was so successful that the company's leaders were dubbed "the whiz kids."

As a part of the "original" leadership team, I was in a position to see firsthand just how extraordinary the future could be for this dynamic company.

We had a great product, a new concept, a charismatic leader in Colonel Sanders, and a well-funded company. Despite all of this, growth proved hard to manage. It was at this point that John Brown decided it was an opportune time to sell the company.

That left those in leadership positions, like me, with the unhappy realization that our future with KFC was limited. If I have learned anything in my professional life, it is this: life is a series of changes.

Let me share with you what happened the first time we met the new boss.

I sat in the board room shortly after the acquisition. The new CEO was presenting his strategy for the first time to those of us who were still left from the old whiz kid gang. It was a closed-door meeting.

Those of us in the old guard were very nervous. We knew things were about to change. Fully aware that the Colonel was no longer running the company, we knew that the culture that we enjoyed so much would soon pass. Inevitably, we knew it was only a matter of time before most of our jobs would also drift up the same smokestack. It was not a question of whether the whiz kids would be replaced; It was a question of when.

The new CEO was tough. During this initial meeting, we thought we would receive at least a little bit of recognition for our part in helping to get the company where it was, which was number one on the New York Stock Exchange. Instead, he just sat there, arms folded. Arrogance. Closed face. No smile. No warmth.

He got right to the point. "Okay, we're going to do things differently around here from now on."

We were stunned and silent. I finally asked, "Like what?"

"Well, for starters, we're going to change the formula of the gravy. We're going to make it with water."

I breathed a sigh of relief that the Colonel was not in this meeting. He was not invited, because The new owners felt his attendance was not needed. As a matter of fact, they believed he was no longer needed, period. He was merely a walking, talking icon; Just one step above the mascot for a sports team.

They would soon learn how wrong they were.

During our meeting, the Colonel happened to walk past the conference room, and saw the light under the door. He stopped and peeked between the two doors and saw the new CEO at the head of the table. Do you know what a closed door meant to the 70-year old Colonel?

Nothing.

He opened the door and walked in. There was a seat next to me, and the Colonel sat down.

"What are they talking about, Frank?"

"Well Colonel, they're going to make some changes."

"What are they gonna change?"

"They're going to change the formula of the gravy."

I think it was at this point that I shut my eyes and prepared for his response.

"Change the gravy!"

"Yes, Colonel."

"What are they going to change?"

"They're going to make it with water," I replied.

The Colonel's eyes flashed as he spun his head in the direction of the new CEO, pointed his finger right at him, and said, *"Don't fool with the gravy!"*

The new CEO said, "Colonel, everything's going to be fine. We've done market research on this and ..."

"Don't fool with the gravy!" the Colonel interrupted, just as emphatically.

The new boss was on the spot. He decided it was an opportunity to show that he was the alpha leader. He leaned forward on the conference table and said, "Colonel, I want to remind you of who's the boss around here. I am the new CEO of this corporation. What I say goes from now on. Do you understand that? Can you get that straight? What you say doesn't matter anymore."

We just waited for the Colonel to fall over in a heap. For about thirty seconds, the Colonel exchanged looks with his successor, processing what had been said. The CEO leaned back, folded his arms, and stared at the Colonel. The Colonel leaned forward and grinned at him! The rest of us were sweating from the palms of our hands, not knowing what would happen next.

The Colonel abruptly got up and headed toward the door.

The CEO said, "Where you going, Colonel?"

The Colonel turned around and looked at him with fire in his eyes, and the hint of a smile in his voice, and replied, "Goin' on the Johnny Carson Show and tell 'em, 'That shit ain't fit to eat!' "

Chalk one up for the Colonel. The gravy stayed the same.

What's the moral of the story? The moral of that story

is simple. *Don't mess with your gravy!*

The gravy represents your people, your employees. They bring it all together. True leaders never miss an occasion to acknowledge the participation of their employees in the success they're having. Real leaders understand success is driven by a dedicated and motivated work force.

Gravy comes in many forms.

It's how you make your employees feel.

The way you treat them.

The way they feel appreciated.

The long-term relationships you form with them.

Your attitude of being the very best your company can be.

Your attitude of being the very best you can be.

Letting them know you think they're the greatest.

Helping them know that you're in their corner.

Showing that you are on the same team.

Demonstrating that you are their coach and their fan.

Their supporter.

Their advocate.

That's the way to make real gravy.

It's not technology that gets you long-term employees or customers. Everyone has technology. Your competitor has or will soon get what you have.

So what differentiates you from the competition? Your employees. It's not your organizational flow charts, your quality awards, or your Internet or intranet solutions. It is your people. If you don't understand that and value that and cultivate that, you will miss the greatest asset you have on the books . . . your human capital. That's your gravy.

Once is Not Enough

Several years ago, I was invited to speak at the annual convention of the Saturn Corporation in Spring

Hill, Tennessee. As you know, Saturn successfully invented and implemented the concept of automobile re-
tailing, with no haggling over price. While address-
ing this group, I shared the story of the Colonel's gravy.

The meeting was for the Saturn retailers. It was also
attended by John Smale, the recently retired chairman of the
board of General Motors, and by my friend, Don Hudler,
who soon afterward became the president of Saturn. They
loved the gravy story, and I was grateful to hear their laugh-
ter and applause.

Years later, I received a call from Don Hudler, now the
president of Saturn. After exchanging cordialities and personal inquiries, I said, "So, Don, what can I do for you?"

"Francis, we need you back up here right away."

"Well, Don, I'm honored. What's going on?"

"To be candid with you, we're messing with the gravy."

It's like anything else important. Gravy requires constant attention. It reminds me of the Irish wife who com-
plained to her husband, "Pat, you never tell me that you love
me."

The husband, never taking his eyes off the game on the
tube, responded, "Maggie, I told you 30 years ago on our
wedding day I loved you. If I ever change my mind, I'll let
you know."

Big mistake.

It's a mistake at home and it's a mistake at work. Life
does not happen in large, epic moments, it occurs in small
slices, a day at a time. It is how we treat each other daily that
determines the big picture of loyalty and morale.

When was the last time you let your employees know
how you felt about them? When was the last time you let
them know that you thought they were the greatest? You
have to make it a daily routine. They have to know that you
believe in them. When problems occur, they need to see

you take the stage; While you're on stage, they need to understand that you are a part of their team, and that they are needed, wanted, and respected.

People—Service—Profit

At FedEx, we had a genuine commitment to three core values — *People, Service* and *Profit*. If you take care of your employees, they'll take care of your customers, and the profit will take care of itself.

Maybe it's too simple for many of us to accept. Leaders focus on their employees. Employees focus on the customer. If leaders and employees are doing their job, the customers will reward them. It works.

Find the right recipe for your company. Then remember: "Don't mess with the gravy."

YOU'RE THE GREATEST

· CHAPTER NINE ·

THE EMPLOYEE'S
ROI

"I LEAVE MY JOB AT THE OFFICE....RIGHT!

During the early days of Federal Express, I hired Bill Catlette as managing director of Employee Relations. Bill and his team helped develop many of the programs which enabled FedEx to earn distinction as one of the nation's Five Best Managed Companies and one of the 100 Best Companies to Work for in America.

He now works as an outside consultant for us at Maguire Communications, developing human resource strategies, policies, and programs for companies worldwide. Bill also takes a lead in our two day *Leadership At The Lake* seminar where leaders learn how to make a difference by improving employee retention, employee and customer relations, and profits. Managers learn such competencies as:

- How to get your employees and customers really *committed*
- How to show them you *care*
- How to *enable* for peak performance
- How to *reduce* employee and customer turnover

It's absolutely vital to be committed to this idea of the employees' ROI. Along with Richard Hadden, Bill wrote a wonderful book everyone in a leadership position should have, *Contented Cows Give Better Milk: The Plain Truth About Employee Relations and Your Bottom Line* (Saltillo Press, ISBN 1-890651-04-4). Catlette makes this point about Employee R.O.I.

If you treat people right, you'll make more money.Whether it's heavy manufacturing, distribution, retail, service, high-tech or professional sports, it is no accident that the organizations consistently identified as winners in their chosen field also happen to be some of the best places on earth to work.

This occurs not as an afterthought, but as a vital, premeditated element of business strategy. It's a relentless truth that those in the unenviable position of having to compete with the likes of Southwest Airlines, GE, FedEx, Hewlett Packard, 3M, Wal-Mart and scores of lesser known organizations have to face every day.

Through a ten year study of employee practices as compared to financial returns, Catlette and Hadden demonstrate that technology, capital spending, and restructuring alone do not lead to the promised land. They present cold, hard facts about the return on investment derived from treating employees with dignity, respect, and consideration. They continue:

Just what is it that permits one organization to achieve unprecedented levels of success over a substantial period of time while a nearly identical competitor is going down the tube!

How, for example, could Southwest Airlines achieve 23 consecutive years of record revenues and profits while TWA, Continental, Pan Am, Eastern, Braniff and others all around them were hemorrhaging red ink?

How could GE, at a plant near Columbia, Tennessee, produce refrigerator compressors at a cost substantially less than that of its foreign competitors, despite an unfavorable cost differential?

The lesson is clear way down to the bottom line of the financial spreadsheet. When you treat people right, you make more money.

Challenges of the New Millennium

There are three challenges in this new century to obtain a return on your investment:

1) The management challenge
2) The employee challenge
3) The leadership challenge

Everyone wants to feel recognized, appreciated, and valued. The idea of making everyone on the team feel the greatest turns philosophy into action. This guarantees the success of your business, the productivity of your employees, and the loyalty of your customers.

The Management Challenge
A sense of urgency must be developed in managers to nurture and support their employees. They must see the need to treat employees with respect and compassion. They must understand that these actions increase employees' tenure, productivity, satisfaction, and profit. Managers must also learn to enhance the workplace through acts of kindness, compassion, empathy, humor and, yes, fun. You don't always have to grit your teeth to manage effectively. Enjoy it! They will, too.

The Employee Challenge
Employees must be convinced that they are the company. They are not manual laborers, but professionals — partners — operating with a sense of the whole company and with knowledge and decision-making power of their own. They must feel needed, wanted, and respected. They must feel good about what they do, who they work for and who they

serve (customers). They must be enabled to create, produce, solve problems, and achieve ambitious company goals.

The Customer Challenge

Corporate America must remain customer driven, customer centered, and customer sensitive. Your customers must feel that you see them. They must understand that you appreciate them and that you are working to make their business a success.

You must give them a reason for continuing to do business with you. Communication is key.
They must hear from you. They must see, hear, and experience who you are, what you do, and how you help them. They must understand this partnership you share for mutual success. Your customer should feel like your employee is on their payroll.

Take Care of Your Customers

Customers want the same thing that employees want from a company; To be appreciated, acknowledged, and understand that you appreciate their business. To know that you are committed to them — truly — to help them succeed. Not just what's on your ad copy. But that you honestly have a relationship with them which you value and honor. That's the exciting part of this premise of You're the Greatest.

You transcend business as we have known it - which too often isn't satisfying and usually isn't successful in creating life-long customers.

Your customers should be your friends. They remain loyal to you because you offer more than just a business relationship. You like them!

It doesn't have to be complicated.

Your employees will model your behavior to your customers, customers will feel appreciated will return, and that's a great R.O.I.

Before and After the Return Comes In

Your ability to validate employees and customers is essential. It will determine your R.O.I. You need to be aware of the tremendous influence you have on others in every area of your life. Here are some specific additional actions you can take:

1) Look them in the eyes.
2) Be fair and consistent.
3) Be kind. Treat others the way you want to be treated
4) Listen.
5) Be patient.
6) Ask for their opinions. Then listen.
7) Look for ways to build them up.
8) Smile
9) Have fun.
10) Help them as people, not as employees or customers.

Life is a series of deposits and withdrawals. You get back what you put in. When you make an investment, you expect a return. When you invest in validating your employees, you want results.

Yet I suggest to you that life's enjoyment and fulfillment are found in the journey—not the destination. Indeed, life is about the journey, not the destination. It's the ability to enjoy the ride, to smell the flowers, to admit that all is not perfect or going according to plan, but you're still able to smile and enjoy where you find yourself and with whom you happen to be — your company, your family, your city or your job.

You Get What You Pay For

The traditional method of deciding how to allocate hard dollars to your capital budget is to determine the R.O.I. What return can you expect from your investment? The question arises, what's a highly motivated and dedicated employee worth?

The first investment, the time you spend to recruit and train your new employees, goes right to the bottom line. Therefore, you must retain your employees. If not, you have to repeat the same initial expense to recruit and train more employees. Finally, you want employees who perform to and above standards each day, or you are in a world of trouble. It pays enormous dividends to be considerate, kind, thoughtful, and nice. Only then do you get exceptional, loyal, and motivated employees.

That's why this whole ideology of making people feel the greatest makes sense. Or should I say cents. People will do amazing things when they feel good about where they work. They produce. They remain loyal. They excel.

This doesn't happen by accident. It requires a concentrated effort. It requires money, time. and attention. The results speak for themselves. Regardless of how you treat your employees, you will get a return on your investment.

These are the people who validated me every day of my life and charted my course, and that of my children and their children. My parents, Emily and Frank Maguire.

A much younger Charlie Osgood and me standing next to John Cavacas. John and Charlie co-wrote the song "Discover America" for President Johnson.

My friend Hubert Humphrey, a man with a heart as big as his body, who tought me the power of validation. He really cared about people.

It's been more than 30 years and Ted and Charlie are two of my best friends. Through the years we have touched each other's lives and I am very grateful to them.

Colonel Sanders taught me the value of a positive attitude in good times and in bad. He never knew how old he was. How old would you be if you didn't know how old you were?

Time flies. Take advantage of it.

In the marketplace in Cairo. colonel Sanders was recognized by people all over the world. And they always felt better about who they were after his visit.

"Big John" Culkin stood by me during the best and worst of times. He never ceased validating my feelings and dreams. I think about him every day.

Celebrated radio personality Al "Jazzbeau" Collins, Tony Bennet, Frank, celebrated New York radio personality William B. Williams, and world famous keyboard players Jay Bushkin and Dave McKenna at Franks surprise 50h birthday party.

Working for the fly-by-night company from Memphis. Little did we know that our company's name would become a verb.

Steve Williford is more than a co-author. He is not only a talented and gifted writer, but a good friend with the gift of validation and perseverance.

Before you realize it, you're looking up to your children. I'm realizing the power of their self-esteem.

My children, Patrick and Elizabeth. Our children are the greatest teachers we will ever have. It is true that the apple never falls far from the tree.

Growing up with your sisters is the best way to find out what love is all about. Here are Margaret Lakis and Virginia Frank with their big brother.

YOU'RE THE GREATEST

· CHAPTER TEN ·

HEARTH

"THE LATIN WORD FOR FOCUS!"

When I left Federal Express, I was looking for a platform to reenter the world of communications. I founded a company called Hearth Communications with a partner by the name of John Culkin. John was like a brother to me, a former Jesuit priest, and as such very fluent in Latin. He showed me how the word, hearth, blended beautifully with our mission in life, which is to have people understand that the most powerful way to get things to happen is to become an effective communicator.

John would often say that communications will be the critical test of the modern world. Not only do I believe that, but I also see that demonstrated more and more every time I go into a client's organization. The root cause of their problems often stem from a *failure to a communicate*. So, John and I built our firm on one concept which is very simple. In Latin, hearth means to *focus*. As we looked at the word hearth more closely, we discovered several vitally important words contained within the word HEARTH:

Ear
Hear
Earth
Heart
Art

I'd like to share my ideas on this word, hearth.

Come Sit by the Fire

When I say hearth, what image comes immediately to your mind? Probably something very positive, inviting, nurturing and appealing. A hearth is a fireplace. It is a source of light, heat, and energy. It's a nice place to drink a cup of coffee, or sit and read a book, hold a conversation, or stare into the flames and think.

When I see the word, I think of a roaring fire with a couple of rocking chairs in front it, and a table between them which holds a few books and a couple of cups of coffee.

That's why I like the image of a hearth. It represents warmth and safety in a time of fear and worry and insecurity. It's easy to get caught up in worry about things we usually have no control over. There's very little we have control over that we worry about, and even less of what we worry about ever comes true. Worry is worship to the wrong god. It's like a swing in a school yard, there's a whole lot of effort, but you don't get anywhere.

The pain of uncertainty is worse than the certainty of pain. Fear is the great paralyzer to you and your employees. We worry about the next project, the next analysts meeting, the next location, or the next job assignment . . . We're too busy worrying, that we cannot work, achieve, or appreciate others.

Instead, we suffer from worry, and stress and the everyday mechanical, interpersonal and personal frustrations of life. We all look for and need sanctuary, a place to get away from it all. A place that allows you to keep or regain your focus. To me, that's sitting in front of the hearth, in the company of those who think you're wonderful.

Well, I have great news. I know of such a place just for you. The best news is, it requires no brick masons, registration fees, or frequent flyer miles. The fact is, you have a hearth inside of you. So do I, I discovered.

Why are you looking *out there*. The answer is not in "if only" land.

"If only I could get away for a few days . . ."

"If only I could get that promotion . . ."

"If only I looked like her (him) . . ."

"If only I wasn't in this predicament!"

The answer, the light, the security, the warmth, the hearth — it's inside of you!

You are the hearth!

Regardless of the circumstances in which you find yourself, you can always keep your focus, because of the hearth which is within you. Part of that focus for you is to make people feel that they are the greatest. The words contained within "hearth" will help you keep your focus.

It's made all the difference in the world for me with the companies I've worked for.

YOU'RE THE GREATEST

· CHAPTER ELEVEN ·

EAR

**"THE SIX LETTERS THAT SPELL LISTEN,
ALSO SPELL SILENT."**

I'll never forget the time that I traveled to the Soviet Union with Colonel Sanders. The Colonel and I were invited to the Kremlin to talk about the production of white protein and its nutritional and economical benefits. At the time, the early 70s, the Russians were struggling with their harvests and feeding their people. Most people didn't know that the Colonel was a nutritional expert. With the approval of the State Department, we went over to help.

Let me set the stage. In Europe, particularly Eastern Europe, the older you get, the more respect you receive, They really put the elderly on a pedestal. If by chance you wore a uniform, or showed a lot of medals, you received much recognition.

The Colonel and I were walking across Red Square on our way to the meeting. It was a Friday afternoon and the doors of the Kremlin opened up and the government workers left to go home to be with their families for the weekend. They were pouring out into Red Square by the thousands.

As they walked, they couldn't help but notice this 75-year-old man—with pure white hair, a white goatee, dressed in a white suit, a black string tie, a diamond pin in his lapel and a jeweled cane—walking across Red Square. To say the least, they were most impressed . . . and curious!

As they walked by, they would smile and stare at us. They gawked and spoke in an excited manner. The Colonel was baffled by this attention. He turned to me and asked, "What are they sayin'?"

I smiled. "Don't worry about it, Colonel. Everything's fine. "We walked a little farther and another group went by, and smiled and mumbled.

"Frank, I want to know," he half-shouted irritably, "what are they sayin'?"

"Everything is fine, Colonel," I assured him, and we

continued on our way to the meeting.

Still another group passed by, same scenario. The Colonel was now getting pretty hot. "Frank, I want to know what they're sayin'."

I said, "Colonel, relax, it's all right. They're just curious."

He snapped, "Do you understand Russian?"

"A little bit," I said.

"Do you know what they're sayin'?"

"Yes, Colonel. I know what they're saying."

"Well, what are they sayin'?"

I thought for a moment and said, "They're asking each other, 'Who is that guy with Frank Maguire?'"

The Colonel thought this was hilarious. Here we were in the one place in the world where nobody knew the world famous icon of chicken.

Everyone needs recognition, even the well-known Colonel Sanders. The Colonel's question is one that I would recommend to you as standard operating procedure when it comes to leadership, before saying anything yourself, first find out what they're saying. Listening before you speak not only prevents you from putting your foot in your mouth, but also is a very powerful form of employee recognition.

Listening is the most under-valued aspect of communication.

The most valuable thing you can do in almost any situation is to listen. If you're managing employees, listen before you speak. You'll have much more information when you do respond. When you make it a habit to listen, you learn the problems, frustrations, and needs of your employees and customers. Listen to their concerns, their fears, and their points of view.

Too many managers have fooled themselves into thinking that employees are dying to hear more of their opinions.

You've heard of the manager who told an employee, "But enough about my opinions, what do you think about me?"

You can't learn if your mouth is open. Shut it and listen.

If you want to succeed, you must first listen. In fact, in order to communicate effectively with anyone, you must first listen. If you take that word, listen, you'll see there's another word within it: silent. The letters that spell the word listen also spell the word silent. Is there a message in there? When you genuinely listen to someone, you validate them instantly. You give them recognition, something we all crave. Even my old friend, Harland Sanders, was in need of recognition.

The Seven Critical Words

Here's a very graphic way to prove the effectiveness of listening. I want you to check these words at the door, and promise never to reclaim them:

That's the way we do it here

Seven simple, often used, totally unproductive words. In fact, they are counter productive. Although there are many reasons why these words are ineffective, a large reason is because they inadequately answer a question instead of encouraging participation in the search for an answer.

Those words convey to the person on the other side of desk, who is asking why something is the way it is, that you are not willing to *listen* to any other opinion. In other words, end of story. They can make you come off as the bad guy, they undercut employee morale, and they rob you of a desirable solution to the problem.

Instead of telling them, "That's the way we do it here," here are the seven magic words that I want you to say the next time somebody comes to you with a problem and asks what to do. I want you to look at them in the eye and say:

'I don't know. What do you think?"

Let me tell you what can happen. There are two possibilities:

1) They were going to tell you exactly what you were going to tell them. But now, it's their idea. They own it. Good for you. They'll more strongly support an idea in which they share ownership.

2) They just might give you an idea you haven't yet thought of. Just because you're the boss doesn't mean you have a corner on the market of good ideas. Leaders listen. Keep it up.

The Seven Percent Solution

Early on at FedEx, we had a familiar personnel problem. Turnover. At the time, Harry Keenen was vice president of personnel. I explained to Harry that the financial people were telling me that we had a problem at the Hub. We had to reduce our turnover. It was getting close to 50 percent. As we have discussed already, it's very expensive to recruit and train new employees.

Harry looked at me, smiled and said, "Okay, Francis, what do you want me to do?"

I smiled, too, and said, "Harry, I don't know. What do you think?"

We talked a little more, and he said, "Let me think it over." A week later, Harry came back and said, "I think I've got the answer, Frank, if you give me what I need." So, I set up a meeting with the CFO, and Fred Smith, CEO and chairman, and me. Harry took the stage and started the meeting. He explained how he took a look around the Hub, spoke to many employees and observed them doing their jobs. Since the launch window (receiving, routing and loading the packages) was so short, they were all part-time employees.

"These employees only work four hours a day. Not during the light of day, mind you, but in the middle of the night," Harry reminded us. "It's not even a full-time job. They have no benefits. I think they feel like stepchildren. They don't feel like they belong in the organization. When it gets to be wintertime, they aren't motivated to work in cold weather. They are college students. When it gets to be exam time, they don't show up.

"And yet these part-time employees, who are mostly college students, are a critical piece to the company. They are the linchpin."

"So what's the answer?" the CFO asked.

"Give them full-time health benefits," Harry replied.

Of course, the immediate concern was the prohibitive cost of adding all those employees to our health plan. He informed Harry that it couldn't be done. The company couldn't afford it. "We can't give part-time employees health benefits. That's not the way we do it here," Pete objected.

Harry said, "Pete, do you know how old the people are who work in Hub?"

"What does that have to do with anything?" he replied.

Harry said, "Most of the employees in the Hub are between 18 and 23. Pete, how sick did you get when you were that age?"

There was momentary silence. I saw Fred smile and say, "Harry's got an idea here."

With the approval of Fred and the common sense of Harry, that's exactly what we did. We gave those part-timers full-time health benefits. Within six months, turnover went from nearly 50 percent to less than 10 percent. The insurance claims were minimal, morale soared, and productivity increased dramatically as our volume continued to skyrocket.

There was another benefit. You couldn't get these guys and gals to quit. They were young and energetic and they liked being able to work at night and go to school during the day. And when they graduated, guess where they wanted to work? You got it. The tradition continues to this day. Many of the people in key management positions today at FedEx began in the Hub as part-timers. That's where they caught the FedEx vision, excitement and values.

And it all came about when Harry was asked, "What do you think?"

Listen to the Heartbeat

Listening allows you to turn off the blinding spotlight of your ego and turn on the floodlights, so we can all see. All of a sudden, you see and understand the big picture.

Listening also communicates the message that you care what others think. You may not always agree with what you hear, but you care enough to listen. We have all seen how listening to someone's problems diffuses the situation. It's like letting air out of a balloon, and all you did was listen. You didn't say anything, you were silent. Why do employees feel better when problems are shared?

Part of the frustration of anyone with a problem is feeling like it's not understood. That they're not heard. That nobody listened. If I have a problem and I tell you and you listened, then I feel much better because you now understand how I feel.

You haven't done anything about it. You don't have to do anything about it. Just know how I feel. I'm much less frustrated and hostile. Now I know that you know, I can think a little more clearly. I'm now ready to hear what you have to say.

Listening is a critical asset for anyone in management. You can't succeed if you don't know how to listen.

It makes you a better team player.
It helps build morale.
It keeps you in touch with the pulse of your employees.
It keeps you in touch with the pulse of your customers.
It helps prevent little fires from becoming infernos.
It makes the work place more enjoyable for everyone.

Think of the friends that you particularly enjoy being with, and think of those friends that you feel are excellent conversationalists. Chances are, it's the same list. Furthermore, when you think more about your conversations with these friends, you'll find that they listen. They allow you, and others, the opportunity to talk.

People who talk all the time are entertaining for only so long!

People who are constantly trying to be witty are fun for awhile, and then it gets old. You soon grow weary of their selfish antics of monopolizing the conversation.

Even people who are extremely intelligent and can talk about anything (and always do) are stimulating to be with for a time, and then it's not enjoyable anymore.

Why?

They're using their mouths, but not their ears. It takes both. As Mose Allison sings, "Your mind is on vacation and your mouth is working overtime."

It pays to listen and be silent. With our friends, with our employees and yes, with our families.

Ready, Aim, Focus

In many ways, we are our own worst enemies.

We keep shooting ourselves in the foot. When we talk and don't listen, we lose our focus or hearth. And if our focus is on being the best we can be, we improve our communication.

We can't enhance our communication until we maximize our listening skills.

By listening, you unleash the potential that exists within your work force. Slashing costs and operating expenses are not the way to increase productivity. You can't think they're the greatest if you're not listening.

Take a look at the people around you. They're going to go home tonight and somebody is going to ask them at the dinner table, "How did it go at work today?" The way those employees respond depends a whole lot on whether or not somebody's listening at work.

Make your organization more productive. Make your employees' family meals more enjoyable.

Listen.

YOU'RE THE GREATEST

· **CHAPTER TWELVE** ·

HEAR

**"REALITY IS IN BEHAVIOR
MORE THAN WORDS."**

I t's important not only to listen (Ear), but also to *understand* (Hear). Unfortunately, too many people never listen and, therefore, have no hope of understanding. In order to be an effective communicator, you must first listen and then understand before uttering the first word. Communication: message sent, message received, message responded to.

To truly hear is a lesson that successful leaders first must learn and then practice. Sadly, it's a lesson that many senior executives and managers have failed to learn.

To *hear* requires active listening. If you don't understand what your employee is saying, ask questions, just to make sure the message you received is what was sent.

As we discussed earlier you listen in silence with your ears, but you hear with your heart. You absorb it. For example, suppose an employee tells you he's doing fine; Your ears received the message, but you can tell from his face, his eyes, his tone of voice, his posture, and his lack of enthusiasm that he's not fine. You didn't discern that with your ears, it came from your heart. Remember what the wise fox said to the little prince. "It is only with the heart that one can see clearly. What is essential is invisible to the eye."

What Makes a City Special?

I was flying back home after giving a speech in New York City. The passenger who happened to sit down beside me was David Brenner, who I, of course, recognized him as the comedian I'd seen countless times on television. He, of course, had no idea who I was.

I didn't say a word to him during the majority of the flight because he was busy and I didn't want to disturb his productivity. As we began our descent, I turned to him and introduced myself. "David," I said, "on behalf of the millions of people who have been made to forget their problems for a little while and share some smiles and laughs with you, allow me to thank you!"

He looked at me for several seconds. Then he said, "Thank *you*. I really needed to hear that just now." He went on to tell me of some personal crises he had been battling for the past several months and shared some of the particulars. Still confiding in me, he told me that one of the reasons he was on that flight was to face a personal concern of his, and that by doing the comedy club circuit, he was able to be in closer touch with his fans, try out new material, and, in many ways, begin afresh.

I told him that so many of us choose to sit around and do nothing and feel sorry for ourselves, and it was refreshing to hear that he was taking action.

He nodded and said, "That's exactly what I'm doing."

I thanked him for sharing a slice of his life with me. Then we said goodbye.

Later that afternoon, I told a friend of mine that I had flown home next to David Brenner. He said that he was a huge Brenner fan, too.

I said, "Well, he's performing right here in Memphis, tonight. Let's go see him."

I picked up the phone, called the comedy club where he was performing, and reserved a table. That entire evening was not only enjoyable, but very memorable. The opening act was fun. The dinner was great.

Then Brenner took the stage and blew the crowd away. We laughed at his stories and, being a public speaker, I marveled at his craftsmanship. Just before he finished his act, he told the audience, "I want to share a story with you. Today, as I was flying into Memphis, I was feeling low. The events of my life in these past few months haven't been very funny.

As a matter of fact, they've been tough on me both personally and professionally.

"But coming in today, I sat next to someone from your city who not only recognized me, but actually thanked me for making people laugh. I was touched. Then he let me share a few of the downers I've been going through. I don't know who he was, but I do remember that he cared. It's people like that that make Memphis the special place that it is to me... and always will be."

My buddy and I just looked at each other. We were moved, Brenner was moved, and so was everybody in the audience. I didn't even try to go back to see Mr. Brenner. As a matter of fact, I never tried to contact him to tell him my name. I'm just glad that I could be the one sitting next to him.

The reason I remember this story is that I really didn't say much at all. I just listened, but I also *heard* what he was saying. He felt it, and it made a profound difference to him that day.

That's what listening and hearing can mean to your employees, your peers and your family. It really makes a profound difference. We all need to feel that we've been heard.

Listening and hearing, the critical links to effective communication. You can't effectively respond to anyone if you don't hear the message.

You can't assume that you understand it.

You can't be thinking about something else while they're explaining it.

You can't think even about that wise pearl of wisdom you're going to blurt out afterwards.

As a matter of fact, you don't have to worry about how you're going to respond at all.

You just have to listen and hear.

People will forget what you say.
People will forget what you do.
But they will never forget how you made them feel.

When you learn that lesson, you have learned how to listen with your heart.

YOU'RE THE GREATEST

· CHAPTER THIRTEEN ·

EARTH

"THERE IS NO SUBSTITUTE
FOR REALITY."

When his company was acquired, Colonel Sanders was asked by the new CEO to bring his original 11 herbs and spices recipe to the office so it could be safely secured in the vault. The Colonel hesitated.

The new CEO said, "You do know the recipe, don't you Colonel?"

"No, I don't know the recipe," the Colonel replied.

"Colonel, I just spent almost half a billion dollars for this company. I'd like to think I bought more than just an old man in a white suit."

The Colonel stared back, thought for a moment, walked over and looked him the eye. He said, "I don't know what you're getting so excited about. It's not the 11 herbs and spices that made this company great. It's the 12th ingredient. The secret ingredient."

The new boss said, "What secret ingredient?"

The Colonel responded with passion, *"You're looking at it!"*

The Colonel's message was clear. It was intended for the new CEO, but it just as easily applies to you and me. We're in the people business. There is no "secret" ingredient that puts us ahead of the competition. There is no silver bullet, no short cut. The harder we work, the luckier we get.

I'm reminded of my friend, Charlie Osgood. Now there's a hard worker. He hosts the Sunday Morning show on CBS. In addition, he writes and narrates the Osgood File radio shows every day on the CBS radio network. Charlie stays perpetually busy, working on one special project after another. People like him who are really successful are people who really work hard. Even those "lucky" folks that you think don't work hard? They do.

Feet Firmly Planted

Just as it is important to listen and to understand, you must also have your feet firmly planted on the Earth. Your thoughts and actions must be based in reality. Simply stated, *never promise more than you can deliver. But always deliver what you promise.* It really is that simple.

It reminds me of a man who sold strawberries at his roadside stand. There was always a line of people waiting to buy his berries because his prices were by far the cheapest in the county.

A friend found out that the man, incredibly, was paying 10 cents more for each carton of berries than what he was selling them for.

"You've got to stop selling this way," his friend urged. "If you don't, you're going to go bankrupt."

The strawberry sultan nodded and said, "I'd love to quit, but business is so good!"

You have to keep your feet on the ground. You can't sell any product or service at a loss and make it up on volume. Despite being aware of this, there are many corporate practices and activities taking place as you read this that are not based in reality. They might as well set up shop with the man at the strawberry stand.

The Book of Dumb Ideas

As a leader, you learn much about reality by listening to employees and your customers. They will tell you what's real, true, and what's important for you to know. Your challenge is to act based upon what you hear.

You must also know what is realistic to ask of your employees. You must know what's within their capacity and what's beyond their reach.

In the workplace, you must be grounded in reality. Our solutions must be grounded in the needs of our customers, employees, and managers. Our goals must be specific; the recommendations must be realistic and the results must be tangible. That doesn't prevent you from being ambitious or creating a new industry. It does help you get there from here.

Effective leaders have to also be able to combine reality with vision. It's not the easiest recipe in the kitchen. What might seem totally unrealistic today is the way business may be defined tomorrow. A few years ago, if one of your employees suggested selling over the Internet, what would your response have been? Today, the Internet is the fastest growing division of sales for a growing number of companies.

When Kemmons Wilson wanted to build a chain of motels along the new interstate highway system across the country where kids stayed free, and the best surprise was no surprise, he had to seek high and low for investors. Everyone said he was crazy, it couldn't be done. The result was Holiday Inn.

When Walt Disney wanted to spend a fortune to make a huge amusement and learning community out of a Florida swamp, many tried to discourage him as others had when he earlier built Disneyland. They told him it was totally unrealistic. Of course, the result was Disney World.

When Herb Kelleher and his partners took on the major airlines to fight for the right to start a small airline company, some of the potential investors he courted just shook their heads. No way. The result was Southwest Airlines.

When Fred Smith suggested he was going to pick up small packages, fly them all to Memphis, shuffle them up and fly them back out, he was told it was an impossible idea. The result was Federal Express.

I've often thought there should be a book of these dumb ideas. I mean, really. Consider the following list of dumb ideas:

Chicken in a box
Overnight Delivery
Pizza in a van
Books on the Internet
Movies on a CD
Phone on your belt
Computer on your lap
A telephone in an airplane

"This will never work."
"It's never been done that way."
"That's not the way we do it here."

Need I say anything else? When people tell you that you have a dumb idea, you ought to pursue it.

The best way to predict the future is to invent it!

The Crucial Connection

It's a matter of connecting your head with your heart. You can have a solid business plan which produces good revenues, and you can have a strong, vital culture of employee validation. They are not mutually exclusive. As a matter of fact, they must go hand in hand. In a healthy business, one cannot grow a business plan over a sustained period of time, without allowing the heart of your company to grow also.

YOU'RE THE GREATEST

· CHAPTER FOURTEEN ·

HEART

"IT IS ONLY WITH THE HEART
THAT ONE CAN SEE CLEARLY."
The Little Prince by Antoine de Saint Exupéry

Federal Express had a hard decision in 1987. We had an electronic mail service called Zap Mail. It was the forefather of the fax machine. Unfortunately, it was unsuccessful. We put many millions of dollars into it, trying to make it work, but the market demand wasn't there yet, and the technical problems were insurmountable. We shut the service down, although we went to great lengths to take care of our customers by providing them alternative equipment at no charge.

FedEx had a very strong commitment to its employees, as indicated by our no lay-off policy. But now, we had over a thousand displaced employees. That's a challenge.

On June 6, 1987, Fred Smith gave a very interesting commencement address at Rhodes College where he reflected on this event.

"By the way, if you know of anyone who happens to need a few thousand facsimile machines, let me know. My wife wants me to get them out of our garage."

Well, in addition to having a few machines left over, we also had about 1,300 people. Our People philosophy was put to the test. We took action to reorganize and find new positions for every one of those 1,300 employees.

Whether we're implementing a new technology or discontinuing an old service, people come first. We in management know that if we treat employees the way we want to be treated, we'll have a more motivated and productive work force.

There's an important message for everyone buried in our Zap Mail experience. The way Federal Express dealt with discontinuing Zap Mail may be one of our strongest moments as a company — because our commitment to both customers and our employees was soundly demonstrated.

We didn't have the right slots for many of those

employees. It was interesting and really, pretty humorous to see employees working in jobs that neither they nor we had ever envisioned them working in. Regardless, their pay checks were never interrupted, And they remember the company's commitment to them to this day.

Fred Smith was leading from the heart.

In an era of depersonalization, adversary management-employee negotiations, downsizing and corporate takeovers, I'm suggesting that you adopt a more personal management style which acknowledges the feelings and *emotions* of your employees as both valuable and fragile. Dedicated employees produce greater earnings.

Successful leaders listen. Successful leaders hear. Successful leaders stay based in reality. But none of this counts if you fail to recognize the importance of coming from the heart. Successful leaders must also lead from the heart.

Great work places are defined less by wages and working conditions than they are by feelings, attitudes, and relationships. Morale and emotions are essential in any successful business. When asked what was the most important thing in winning a war, General Eisenhower replied . . .

"Morale."

No question, *you gotta, have heart!*

As a leader, you must acknowledge your heart. Your heart manifests itself in many ways. These ways are somewhat controversial in some management camps, but you will never be the leader you can be if you don't communicate from the heart.

As a leader, you need to respond intuitively. Listen to that inner voice, pay attention to your gut feeling. Show people that you care about them. Because your employees don't really care how much you know until they know how much you care. That is a real key to a motivated, dedicated work force. Your people need to know that you're coming from the heart.

Let's talk about your inner voice. I'm not talking about a knee-jerk impulse. There are many moments when your inner voice clearly tells you how you should act. Nobody expects you to be perfect. It's not a matter of being right or wrong. It's a matter of caring. . . It's listening to and leading from the heart.

When I hired and did not fire Ted Koppel, I was operating from that place in the heart. Instead of celebrating with my colleagues the signing of the new FAA bill, I chose to listen to an employee tell me about how upset he was about being cut from a company basketball team, I was operating from the heart. When Fred Smith kept every Federal Express employee on the payroll when Zap Mail was dissolved, he was operating from the heart. When Dave Longaberger gave employees a second chance, he was operating from the heart.

When you think about it, most daily activities are not right or wrong. It's more about sincerity and caring. For employees, it's knowing that the leader cares and is leading from the heart. That's someone they can be loyal to. That's leadership.

How do leaders show heartfelt leadership? First of all, they listen, and truly hear what's being said and understand what's going on. Then they stand with both feet on the earth, always staying in touch with reality. Of course, sometimes leaders must discern what reality is. They sometimes have to make decisions against the advice of others. Leaders share in the burden and in the victory. Leaders who lead from the heart are humble and savvy enough to realize that it's a team effort that achieves success.

In all the years I worked for him, I never saw Fred Smith receive an award without saying, "On behalf of the employees of the Federal Express Corporation, I accept this award." And he meant it and means it. The company has been more productive because of his attitude. There is no question about it. A caring company produces more motivated workers, higher earnings and increased profits.

The Head-Heart Connection

The common business modus operandi revolves around thinking and leading with the head. There is a better way. Great leaders lead with their heart, and employees will follow.

As I said, people don't care how much you know until they know how much you care. As a leader who cares, you must really care about the employees. Do you really care? Think about your own employees for a minute. Let me give you a little quiz.

Do you know their names?
How many kids do they have?
Boys or girls?
How are they doing in school?
How old are they?
What's their spouse's name?
How did his/her operation turn out?
Where do they live?
How's the new car running?
What's their passion?
When's the last time you complimented them?

How did you do? The bad news is that if you don't know the answers to most of these questions, you're missing the boat. You are not truly leading from the heart if you don't really know your employees. The good news is, you can change. You need to get to know who they are. Let them know that you really do care about them. Let them know who you are. You have to lead with the heart as well as with the head.

Leading from the heart is not complicated. It doesn't require a great deal of new knowledge. It does require a great deal of heart, consistency in caring, and a commitment to your employees that goes beyond the balance sheet. Once you consistently demonstrate that type of heart-based leadership, you will experience dedication and productivity that exceeds all logical expectations.

That's your ticket to achieving your corporate goals. That's what differentiates your company from others. That's what keeps your staff from leaving. That's what everyone is looking for.

It's more than just a job. It's a place where everybody knows your name. It's a place where others are interested in you. In a world of employee shortages, it's a place where others want to work. It's a place where customers are taken care of, because the employees are taken care of.

It's not about motivation, it's about validation.

YOU'RE THE GREATEST

· **CHAPTER FIFTEEN** ·

ART

"MANAGEMENT IS A SCIENCE,
LEADERSHIP IS AN ART."

Robert Fulghum said, "Everything I Need to Know, I Learned in Kindergarten." I agree. I was speaking to 22,000 automotive workers at the Dallas Convention Center at the annual National Auto Congress. These were people who paint cars and fix fenders and manufacture and supply parts for a living. I said to them, "Remember as a young child, when your mom said, 'We better hold hands, and look both ways, because we are crossing the street."

We are crossing the street. Call it a millennium. Call it a century. We are crossing into a whole new era. The world is changing dramatically and quickly. We better review our old behavioral traits. It is no longer acceptable to just throw people at problems, or throw money at people.

And then I really threw them a curve. I asked them to stand up. Then I asked them to take the arm of the person on each side of them. You could have heard a pin drop. Slowly they locked arms. Finally all 22,001 of us were linked together.

The effect was dramatic. Some laughed. Some cried. Some swayed. Some talked. Some sang. Some danced.

Then I said, "We have to learn to hold hands and look both ways. Because we truly are crossing the street together.

"We are different, but we are a team. And as leaders, you must learn to embrace that diversity and acknowledge that leadership is truly an art. It's as different as there are people in your plant. It's as new as your newest employee.

"Leadership is not stagnant. It's constantly adapting to your employees, your customers, your company and your goals. It requires vigilance, creativity and energy. It also requires perseverance."

Then I told them they could release arms and sit down.

But when they let go of each other, they remained standing. Then a huge ovation erupted, complete with whoops and yells. It wasn't for me. It was for each other. For the team.

Through the years, people have failed to distinguish between management and leadership. Management is a cognitive process. A linear sequence. How do you solve a problem, make a decision or plan? How do you gather, organize and analyze information? How do you manage by objectives? Management is a science. It's measurable. It is needed to determine effectiveness, productivity and problem-solving.

On the other hand, *leadership* is an art. You cannot measure people. You can't weigh them, stack them, and count them, because each one of them is different. A real leader sees not just performance, but also individual potential.

In decades past, everybody needed to be the same. Today, a leader must recognize and celebrate diversity, because the make-up of today's employee pool is very diverse. At FedEx, I was very pleased to see that although we had many employees from deep within the South, many of the people who made major contributions to the launch of the company were from faraway lands like India, the Philippines, the United Kingdom and Australia. Fred Smith didn't just hire people who looked like him and thought like him.

It's ironic that in this age of high technology, creating relationships is an art. As John Culkin, my dear friend and partner, used to say, "we carry our treasures in fragile containers."

Although we share many similarities, we have many more differences. What makes life exciting are those differences.

We're a quilt, not a melting pot. We come from different backgrounds, hometowns, educational experiences, good times, bad times, and careers. We have different accents. We're all ages. We have varied musical tastes. Our skin is different colors and there is so much more that makes each one of us different from the other. That is what has made us the greatest nation the world has ever known.

I can't think of any step-by-step procedure in human relations that would allow for such variables. That's why you have to view communication not as a science, but as an art.

As Buckminster Fuller pointed out, "We are all together on this great spaceship Earth and there are no passengers. We are all crew."

Just think about that for a second. That's true of the corporate world. That's true of your family. That's true of any organization. There's no room for passengers. Everyone has to accept their responsibility and do their job.

I'm not suggesting a step-by-step program for how to be a leader instead of a manager. I just want you to grasp the concept. It's more than formulas and procedures. It's about people. When you recognize that fact, you must acknowledge that a person cannot be measured the way you measure a thing, because a person is a complex entity composed of many variables which have to be considered. It's not simply a matter of behavior.

As an effective leader, you can't simply measure performance without taking into consideration the variables of an employee's life. For instance, an employee may have sick child at home or a sick parent in the hospital.

Leadership is an art as much as medicine, ministry, architecture, coaching, teaching or painting is an art. The management concepts you learn must be applied to your particular situation which includes employees, goals, type of work, season, customers, work environment and compensation.

Looked at as an art, leadership can adapt to the situation. It can constantly improve, and it can be people not procedures focused.

Leadership is not a sprint. It's a marathon. Actually, it's

much longer. I often remind myself, "This is not a dress rehearsal." It is also not the finish line. There is no finish line. You will never "have arrived." We must continually improve upon our abilities to lead. The journey has just begun.

YOU'RE THE GREATEST

· CHAPTER SIXTEEN ·

A CRITICAL
DISTINCTION

**"WE SEE OTHERS AS WE ARE,
NOT AS THEY ARE."**

Have you ever had a strong opinion about a certain subject that you just knew was right? You were so sure that you were willing to bet the farm on it? Then, a moment in time came face to face with incontrovertible evidence that proved you wrong?

We know so much. Yet, as we get older, we discover we realize very little. Knowledge versus realization, a critical distinction in life.

Years ago, I took my daughter, Elisabeth, to Hawaii, on a business trip. That first night, we stood on the shore of Maui, and watched the sun go down over the horizon. It was an awesome sight. I said to Lib, "I thought I knew what a beautiful sunset was, but look at that! I never realized how special a sunset could be until this very moment!"

That experience caused me to think about all those other things I thought I knew.

Being a father.
Receiving a college diploma.
Missing your folks.
Falling in love.
Winning a prize.
Going home.
Getting to a quiet place.
Having a friend.

In short, I came to the realization that knowing and realizing are not the same.

For example, you may be confident that you know how to outthink the other guy. Maybe it's not about outthinking the other guy. It's about thinking for yourself and about all of your employees thinking the same. The real accomplishment not outsmarting your competition, but rather giving your best effort and being a real team.

Finishing best is often better than finishing first.

As a young man, I attended a retreat outside my then hometown of New Orleans. An old seasoned Jesuit Priest gave us a thought or two to contemplate as we began the weekend. I have carried what he said with me ever since. He suggested to us:

In order to be fulfilled in this world, you first need to learn to distinguish between knowledge and realization. We are full of knowledge. We know a lot of things. But when you become involved personally, then, and only then, you realize how much you were mistaken.

I call that phenomenon, *awareness*. I thought I knew what it was like to be a parent. I had friends who were parents. I had parents of my own. Then one day, July 25, 1973, the doctor placed this beautiful, moving creature in a soft blanket, and put her in my arms, and I realized for the first time what it was like to be a parent. Elisabeth Maguire, my daughter, came into my world, and I was never the same.

We can all relate to that, can't we? You think you know what your employees are going through, and then one night you spend a day on the road, or a night in the hub, or a morning on the assembly line. Then you realize. I have a good friend, Harry Chandis, who was president of Continental Airlines. I met Harry at American Airlines, where we worked together. Harry tells about the day he reported for duty at American Airlines. The first thing he told his boss was that he'd be back in two weeks. His boss laughed and said, "What do you mean? This is your first day on the job!"

Harry smiled back and replied, "I know. I'm going out to the airport, put on a pair of jeans, and handle the luggage. Harry wanted to truly understand what was going on at the airport. He didn't want to read a report about it. Reports don't always reflect reality. Managers and employees don't always reflect the complete picture. True leaders have been there and revisit the trenches, often. They have more than knowledge. They have realization.

Opportunity IS NOWHERE
It All Depends on How You See It

The Colonel's office was right on the main floor. Everyone who came to visit the KFC headquarters could see the man if he was in town.

I remember my first visit. Here I was, the newest VP, about to meet the Colonel. He was sitting behind his desk. He looked up, smiled, and invited me to take a seat. As we talked, I couldn't help but notice the sign hanging on the wall behind his chair: *Opportunity Is Nowhere*.

I asked him about the sign, and he asked me to read it. I said, *"Opportunity is nowhere."*

"Are you sure?" the Colonel asked.

I looked at it again and said I was sure.

"To me, it says Opportunity is *Now* Here!" he said.

He was right on target. Same sign, two points of view. That's the way life is.

The truth of the matter is opportunity is now here. There's never been more opportunities to grow. There's never been a better time to achieve, produce, and enjoy. Conditions aren't perfect. The fact is, it's not a perfect world. There will always be problems and challenges. Even in these bountiful times, you can't make everyone happy, no matter what you do. It's the difference between facts (what is) and the future (how you see it). It's the challenge of looking at the world around you and seeing the opportunity. It's the ability to transcend knowledge to realization.

You and I know there is opportunity today. It can be

done. We need to wake up! Realize it. Too many of us have been sleeping. Remember, "It is only with the heart that one can see clearly." You don't need a Harvard Business School degree. The time has come to wake up. Life is in session. When your employees are motivated, opportunity is now here. When employees feel unappreciated, opportunity is nowhere!

It's the little things: A mechanic misses part of the repair order — a missed opportunity.

A manager passes an employee without a word — a missed opportunity.

A flight attendant ignores an equally tired passenger — a missed opportunity.

The CEO is rarely seen by employees — a missed opportunity.

They Missed An Opportunity — Me!

No company can ever be any better than the point of contact employee.

We see this everyday a service driven economy. I'm constantly surprised when I observe employees who are in the service industry and yet not understand how significant they are to the customer. When you come right down to it, to that customer looking at you across the counter you are the company. Employees need to understand that.

A good example of that can be seen frequently and airport when everybody from the ticket agent to the flight attendant walks from one end of the airport to the other representing every single employee who works for the company. It is not the CEO or the vice president who represents the company; It is the individual employee who looks you in the eye and makes you feel good about who you are. Not long ago, I journeyed to Denver from Los Angeles on the flight that was scheduled to, and indeed did, depart at 6 o'clock in the morning. It was a perfect opportunity for everyone to contribute to the chaos and confusion you might expect.

That was not the case for one employee by the name of Maxine Anderson. Maxine worked for American Airlines behind the ticket counter looking out over at thousands of faces wanting only one thing, and that was getting on an airplane. As I approached the counter, I noticed one thing before anything else, that Maxine was smiling. I heard Maxine singing. I received a smile from Maxine as well as a happy "good morning sir". All of a sudden, my day had taken and decided turn for the best. I stood there and showed her my ID, and gave her my flight number, she happily engaged to me in a conversation designed to make me feel good about who I was in the middle of all that chaos. Inside of five minutes I had my upgraded ticket, my gate number, and directions to the gate from a smiling employee. It literally changed my entire day. What airline I'm going to call the next time I have to get on a journey? Thank you, Ms. Anderson, for wonderful day a wonderful smile and a wonderful attitude. That positive story took place at the Los Angeles International Airport, famous for its confusion, long delays, and negative reactions.

The same is true when your apply negative attitude. It is frustrating when you confront an employee of a company with whom you are trying to spend money and receive a negative reception. I am constantly amazed at how so many employees don't understand their role. Do they realize how they impact the customer? Do they realize that all of the knowledge and training they have acquired is for one purpose: of serving the customer?

The word "customer" is derived from the Latin word custom and is defined as a relationship, built on faith, over a long period of time.

It is really no big mystery

Help them to see the big picture. Help them realize that everything they do, regardless of their job, is to help the customer. When they realize that, then special requests from customers or management begin to make more sense. They are able to realize why it's important to respond. Everybody wins. In three short words — *Whatever It Takes.*

Dreams Do Come True

My friend and colleague, Steve Williford, has a plaque in his office which reads, *Happy are those who dream dreams and are willing to make them come true.* I believe that if you can imagine it, you can achieve it. You'll see it when you believe it.

Yes, opportunity is all around us. You simply have to open your eyes and decide what you're willing to commit to. You would not have the idea if it weren't possible to achieve it. It would be impossible to have the thought if you didn't have the power to make it happen.

The truth is, we set our sights too low. When you put your sights too high, the risk of failure is not nearly as great in the long run as when you set your sights too low. Charles Osgood, wrote a poem which spells out what I mean. It's a poem about a bird who never realized who he was.

The Eagle and the Chicken

A man once found an eagle's egg,
and put it in the nest of a barnyard hen.

The eagle hatched,
and grew up with the rest of a brood of chicks.

He thought he didn't look at all the same. He
scratched the ground for worms and bugs, and he
played a chicken's game.

The eagle clucked and cackled..
He made a chicken sound..

He flapped his wings,
but he only flew some two feet off the ground.

That's high, as chickens fly, the eagle had been told.

And one day, when the eagle was quite old, he saw
something magnificent flying very high, making
great majestic circles up there in the sky.

He'd never seen the likes of it. "What's that?" he
asked in awe.

As he stared in wonder and amazement at the grace
and beauty that he saw.

"Why, that's an eagle," someone said..
"He belongs up there. It's clear.

"Just as we, since we are chickens, belong earth bound down here."

The old eagle just accepted that. Most everybody does.

And he lived, and died, a chicken.
Because that's what he thought he was.

Now, there's a lesson in this story, in case you didn't guess. So don't you cry for the old eagle or the mix up with the nest.

For the power of an Eagle, and the strength to soar the sky, is a gift that's born in each of us, if only we will try.

So raise your chin, my little one, and spread your wings to fly, and like the mighty Eagle, make your circles in the sky.

You CAN Get There From Here

I often have that thought when I get on a plane in Los Angeles and head for the East Coast. I'm sitting in the airplane, eating a meal, being served by a friendly flight attendant. And I think that only two or three generations ago, it would have taken my ancestors a year to make this trip, with much hardship. If you had said to them, "Someday, you'll be able to get in a metal tube, sit down, eat, and in four hours be on the other side of this country," they'd have said you were crazy.

Yet those flying tubes are a part of everyday life for us. We must realize that the future is full of exciting possibilities.

Where will you be when you get to where you're going?. . Think about it for a minute. The question will start to make sense. In other words, where do your goals and dreams take you? What is on the other side of your ambitions?

Perhaps it's a cottage on the beach or a cabin in the mountains. Maybe it's being a corporate executive or finally having time to travel.

Each day, I get up and drive over to the swim club and do my laps. I'm eating a much healthier diet and have dropped a significant amount of weight. It was a goal. As was to live where we live. I wanted to do and be the things that made me happy. You can, too. Life really is in session. This is no dress rehearsal.

We always think about how life could be. We think about a new car, new clothes, or a larger house. But let me resubmit the question to you: Where will you be when you get where you're going? Can you tell me at least three goals for your life? Two? One? Remember the words of that great philosopher, Yogi Berra, "If you don't know where you're going, any road will get you there!"

If you're like most people, you can't name a single goal for your life! Isn't that amazing? Even those who knew from age two what *occupation* they wanted to pursue can't tell you what they want to *accomplish* in life.

We labor over projections and directions for our business but can't even list *three* goals for our life! We spend more time planning a vacation than our life!

A salesman from the city, hopelessly lost in the back roads of a rural community, took his map into a small general store to get directions. The store owner looked at the salesman's destination, winked at his friends, and said, "You can't get there from here."

That's the way we think sometimes, isn't it? I can't get there from here, so why try? One thing's for certain. If you don't create a target, you can't aim for it. Remember Whittier's statement? "The saddest words of sword or pen are these, 'it might have been.'"

My first suggestion is don't be afraid to dream.

Second, develop a Polaroid picture. Here's where you are and there's where you want to be. Now, how do you get from here to there? *Some* goals require much time and effort. Are you willing to pay the price?

Third, don't be afraid to fail. The fact is, there is no failure. Failure is not an option. You may come up short, but if you have put out the effort, you haven't failed. I learned from my mistakes and they helped me get to where I am now, and my journey has just begun.

If you're worried about failing, get over it! It's far better to try than to be afraid to try. In other words, if you don't try then you can't grow. Set your compass. Determine the cost. Don't be afraid to fail. Don't even think "fail."

To Risk

Life is not measured by what you achieve, but by the way you deal with challenge. There will always be setbacks en route to your goals, but you can learn from your mistakes and try again. Dreams can, and do, come true.

Greenville was a little more creative in the way he phrased it, but the meaning remains the same.

Opportunity knocked at the door.
Courage answered and let him in.
Interest inquired as to the nature of his business.
Caution asked to see his credentials.
Logic debated where and when such a thing should
be done and who could do it.
But Faith said, "When do we start!"

Your employees have the same needs as you do. There is no limit to what they can achieve if someone who they respect believes they can. Everyone reacts in a positive way when people they look up to and respect believe in them and urge them on. That can be the grease that makes the corporate bureaucracy work. It can make the difference when times are very tough and there simply is no money. This validation helps employees realize not just know they are valued and their jobs are important.

Maybe it's just one small branch of one division where one manager is practicing this type of validation. Often, it's enough to turn on a light that helps illuminate the whole corporation.

One leader with a light in his eye, puts light into others, and can light up an entire organization, because people respond to validation.

> There are no exceptions to this Maguire Absolute:
> If you're my boss and you believe in me . . .
> I'll prove you right.
> But if you have no faith in me . . .
> I may also prove you right.
> There is more power in negativity than we realize.

YOU'RE THE GREATEST

· CHAPTER SEVENTEEN ·

SOONER OR LATER WE WILL ALL SIT DOWN AT THE BANQUET TABLE OF CONSEQUENCES

"YOUR EMPLOYEES WILL TREAT YOUR
CUSTOMERS EXACTLY THE WAY
YOU TREAT THEM."

Everyone likes to think that their job is important. In fact, their job is the most important job in the company. I don't care what department they are in or how much they earn.

Everyone feels that way, or at least they should. The fact is, they are right. All of them!

My very first job was delivering newspapers for the *Long Island Star Journal*. Mr. Little was my first boss. In the storefront where the papers were delivered, he would stack the papers, count them, and distribute them to us kids who would fold them, put them in our bags, mount our bikes, and deliver the papers. We peddled our routes throughout our neighborhood. If I do say so myself, I really threw a great "double" for those buildings having two families residing in them.

I learned, even at this early age, not to underestimate the power of those having the most insignificant positions. I might have just been tossing the papers, but even though those papers were written and printed, until I delivered them, they didn't say a thing.

Employees at all levels are important members of the team. A company is only as strong as its weakest employee. Employees do a better job when they have a reason to. When they feel appreciated, they are more productive.

When Mr. Little spent a little more time with us paper boys, we were more motivated to deliver and collect. If Mr. Little's manager had spent more time with him, he would have been more motivated to spend more time with us. Appreciation and validation have a cascading effect to the front line.

At the Federal Express Corporation, we used to have yearly meetings with all our employees from every single work group. We called them "Family Briefings." As a matter of fact, FedEx was the first corporation to televise its corporate meetings via satellite to its field organizations.

I remember one year in particular. I had assembled a panel of employees, seated around a table. The first one to speak up was a pilot, who alluded to the fact that he flew a multi-million dollar asset, a very significant role in the big picture of the company. He went on for some time. The customer service agent interrupted and gently reminded the captain that if she didn't answer the phone, the plane would not be needed.

Then the courier chimed in, "You guys can argue all you want, but until I pick up that package, the company has nothing to ship." The mechanic said, "If I don't keep the plane in the air, we're out of business." And on it went, all the way around the room. Until all of a sudden, everybody realized that the person who had the most important job in the company was *each one* of them. If one person drops the ball, everybody else loses.

We need to make sure that each one of the people who work in our organizations recognize, realize and believe that he or she has the most important job in the company. It has nothing to do with title or salary. It has everything to do with teamwork.

Each person should hear us tell him or her that on a regular basis. It helps develop pride and validation. It helps create understanding for why it's important to give their best effort every day. Even when no one is looking, it enables the employee to build pride in the company's growth and profitability.

An Attitude of Gratitude

I've watched and observed many leaders. Although I've been around some household names in people and companies, it's taken me awhile to realize what defines a successful leader.

In so doing, I had to come to grips with who I am. I am a lover of people, a husband, a father, a friend who has his share of faults, but a loyal friend to many. I'm a dreamer. I'm imaginative. I'm musical. I communicate well. I invest emotionally. I make people feel good about themselves.

Do I have weaknesses? You bet. Don't put me in charge of your accounting department. I'm not an analytical thinking person. If I had my chance to look in the rearview mirror, I'd probably do a lot of things differently. But I had to learn to accept who I am before I could grow.

I'm one of a kind — like you.

Remember, once again, the wisdom of the fox who came out of the forest and said to the little prince, "It is only with the heart that one can see clearly. What is essential is invisible to the eye."

What is essential about you is not the car you drive, the clothes you wear, the money you have in the bank or the kind of car you drive. What really defines you is the light behind your eyes. The light of enthusiasm. The world is lucky you're here!

In other words, we all have strengths, we all have weaknesses, but this is who we are. Until you accept and like yourself right where you are, you will not enjoy life nor its journey. *And to the extent you accept and like you determines how effectively you can help anyone else along the way, personally or professionally.*

You can't fake it. That doesn't mean you won't have moments of anxiety or doubt. Everybody does. But great companies are the result of people who feel good about themselves. Total self-confidence with grace and dignity (not to be confused with arrogance). Being the *greatest* means being able to obtain a measure of happiness, and that comes without walking around being bitter or angry.

I call it the attitude of gratitude. It's the ability to get up in the morning and be grateful to be alive. Even when things don't go as planned.

People First

In the search for our excellence, it's important not to overlook our most valuable resource. Not a "zero defects" system, not a "Total Quality Management System," not an incentive program or a new marketing campaign. Our most valuable resource is people.

You help them not by motivating, but validating. An incentive program works only about as long as it takes to get back from the reward trip, or wear out the nice pen set. Then employees revert, unless you have a full-time manager dedicated to thinking up the next incentive program.

I'm not against those plans completely, because rewards are often times necessary in the workplace. However, validating an employee is so much more powerful than motivating. When you validate an employee's worth and contribution to the company, you don't have to wave a carrot in front of him, and you don't have to put a manager in front of him. As a matter of fact, he's going to work even harder when the boss isn't around.

We in management, in particular, are probably totally convinced that our companies must provide 100% service. The real trick is *communicating* that goal to our employees. The catch is that we can communicate that goal all we want, but if our employees don't buy into it, if our employees don't operationalize our commitment by making it their *own* commitment, then nothing *will happen*. If this is the case, nobody's goals will be met. The company and the customer will both lose.

The real question isn't whether or not service or customers are important, but *how can we make sure that every single employee will make things happen*?

I'm quite sure we at Federal Express didn't have all the answers. But we tried to create an organization whose culture, philosophy and programs provided an environment in which the highly motivated people who came to us for employment stayed highly motivated, dedicated and productive.

Fortunately, we learned a long time ago that customer relations always begin with employee relations.

Many companies say they're "people companies" and don't do anything to support their claim — lots of talk and no action.

Federal Express' challenge, just like every other company that espouses a people first philosophy, was to make that philosophy *real — in every employee's daily work experience.*

We discovered that if we treated our people with respect and dignity, they would provide a high level of service to our customers - whose business yielded profit for the corporation. However, putting that somewhat ideal, esoteric philosophy into practice meant that we must look at a multitude of ways to replace talk with action.

You can *talk* all you want about "People First," but unless people see it *demonstrated* on a regular basis, it will mean very little. That philosophy must permeate everything you do.

Respect for the dignity of your people demands that you do some very basic things. In fact, they're the *same* things you try to do for your customers: listen to them, discover what they need and give it to them if at all possible. I think employees' needs are simple and universal.

Job security is at the base of any employee's needs.

Quite simply, people need to know that their job is not going to disappear at the whim of management as a last ditch effort to improve the company's profits. We had a great opportunity to back up the rhetoric of our no layoff philosophy at Federal Express.

As I mentioned, when senior management decided to discontinue ZapMail service, 1,300 people's jobs were affected, but no one lost their job. We reorganized and absorbed virtually every person into the work force.

The financial loss related to ZapMail was substantial and probably could have been reduced if we had given 1,300 people two weeks notice. But the decision was management's and every one of those people had worked tirelessly to make ZapMail succeed. There was no way we weren't going to make good on our no layoff philosophy.

We are, or at least we'd better be, people driven. As Fred Smith said, people come in two very important forms in any company: first and foremost are our customers and first and foremost are our *employees. There can be no second place when it comes to people.*

YOU'RE THE GREATEST

· CHAPTER EIGHTEEN ·

THE POWER OF
A THUMBS UP

**"I FEEL GOOD ABOUT ME
WHEN I'M AROUND YOU."**

One of the most pleasant feelings or surprises we share in common is when someone we know tells us of a remark or gesture of generosity a long time ago that made a difference in their life. Sometimes, a very big difference.

I was so pleased to recently receive a call from Charlie Osgood's office, explaining that he was on the cover of the latest edition of *Guideposts Magazine*, and his secretary wanted me to have some copies. I was curious and eagerly awaited to see the magazine. When I received my copies, sure enough, there he was on the cover, with an article entitled, *Be Yourself*. The subtitle was, "You see him on TV while you're getting ready for church. You've heard his voice on the radio for years. Now read about the surprising way he got his start in broadcasting."

As I sat down to read about my friend, my curiosity turned into surprise. Here's part of the article, written by Charlie. He had just explained how he was fired as general manager for the first experimental pay-television station in the United States, "an idea whose time had not yet come."

While I looked for a new job, my wife and I moved in with my parents in New Jersey. I got rides into New York City with Dad's car pool. He was a textile executive. I was an unemployed pay-television tycoon. That's because there wasn't any pay television except at the station I'd been fired from.

I wasn't even sure what kind of work I was looking for. A couple of months passed and I began to wonder if I'd ever work again. This was not exactly my peak of self-esteem. I'd see panhandlers on the street and identify strongly with them. I thought, There but by the grace of God, go I. Speaking of the grace of God, one day I ran into an old friend from Fordham University on the street. Francis X. Maguire had worked with me at the college radio station. He had a job selling jingles. Frank had even tried to sell me a jingle when I was running the pay-TV station in Hartford. But now, he was working, and I wasn't. So he gave me a few names of contacts, and even went with me to see some New York broadcasting executives.

Believe it or not, a few weeks later, my old friend Frank became a New York broadcasting executive himself. ABC Radio hired him to co-produce a new show called Flair Reports. For on-air talent, they were looking to hire five or six people to do news sidebars. Since they wanted to be new and different, they didn't want people with a lot of news experience. I certainly qualified for that.

Frank urged me to come by the next week for an audition. "Write something and bring it in," he said.

"What should I write!" I asked. I'd never written more than a business letter.

*"Write about whatever interests you," Frank told me. **"Be yourself."***

In the New York Times, I found what I thought was the perfect story. It was an obituary of a 100-year-old former Metropolitan Opera diva. She had last sung half a century, half a lifetime ago. I did my best to rough out some copy. At my audition, I read the story into the microphone, feeling as if my mouth were full of cotton. I could see the producers in the control room. Frank was the only one smiling. The others looked at me with No in their eyes. What did they care about a dead diva?

I left the studio dejected, knowing that I just done a terrible audition and blown a good opportunity. Frank caught up with me as I was walking down the hall. He looked me right in the eye and said, "You're hired. I know you can do this." His colleagues didn't want to hire me, but Frank had insisted. He knew what I could do, even if they didn't. Even if I didn't.

The same day, he also hired a 23'year old desk assistant from a local radio station, who hadn't been allowed on the air there even once. Frank was a pretty good judge of talent, though. The kid was Ted Koppel.

Anyway, that's how I went, at age 30, from being one of the youngest TV station general managers in the country to being its oldest cub radio reporter. I stayed at ABC doing Flair Reports and hourly newscasts for five years. And then on to CBS.

That chance meeting so many years ago on the street in New York City began a stellar broadcasting career for Charlie, culminating with his present job as host of Sunday Morning on CBS. Never underestimate the power of a thumbs up!

Would You Please Give Me Back My Weekend?

I've been around many powerful leaders. On the surface, they looked completely secure. You would never guess there was even one ounce of fear, but my experience has also convinced me that no matter what your title or position in life is, we all, no exceptions, carry our treasures in fragile containers.

As a senior officer in more than one major corporation, I made it a point of communicating with my boss, who was usually the CEO. Take Fred Smith, for example. On my way home on Friday afternoons, I'd drop by his office, give him the high sign and say, "See you Monday, Fred. Have a great weekend!"

More often than not, he said, "Yeah, okay, Frank. You have a great weekend, too. See you Monday, and, thanks for going the extra mile this week. It's really paying off." I would hit the elevator with a smile on my face, get in my car, go home, and have a great weekend. You bet I would! It was a grand feeling to be validated at the end of a long, hard week.

I had a great weekend, my kids had a great weekend. Even Thor, my trusty black lab, had a great weekend.

But every once in a while, I was greeted by the thundering sound of silence from Fred's office. On my way to the elevator, I heard, "Frank."

"Yes Fred?"

"I want to see you first thing, Monday morning." No smile. No thanks. Just "first thing, Monday morning."

What kind of a weekend do you think I had? You're right. I had a lousy weekend; Not only me, but my wife, my kids, even Thor, the wonder dog. We all had a miserable weekend. Why? Because all I could think of was "Monday morning," and not knowing what it held. Leadership at home is linked directly to leadership at the office.

Then, after dreading the arrival of Monday, when it was finally time for the meeting, I would ask, "What did you want to talk to me about?" And I would hear, "Oh, I forgot. It wasn't important."

Maybe not to you, but would you please give me back my weekend!

What's the lesson to be learned? Whether you're the CEO, the dad, the mom or the coach you should never underestimate the role that you play in the lives of those around you. Never let anyone in your charge leave for their weekend feeling uncertain or insecure, even employees who might be performing marginally.

We all need joyful, fun weekends. Be aware of that . . always.

It's not a matter of perfection. Certainly none of us has a hope of achieving that. Rather, it's an awareness of those exce-lent qualities in all of us. Not every single issue is a matter of life or death. People crave validation and recognition, just like you. We must be aware of our significance in the lives of others. For like you and me, each of them is carrying their treasures in fragile containers.

We Cannot Not Communicate

Communication is the critical test of our leadership. As a matter of fact, we cannot *not* communicate.

> We do it by our presence, and by our absence, by our silences as well as our words, by our choices, gestures, and attitudes. We may not always do it well, but we always do it.

Think about it for a minute. If you don't show up for a meeting, what message does that send? Something else was more important. If you sit, looking bored and unresponsive during a family gathering, what message does that send to others? Silence speaks much more loudly than words.

Have you ever sat in a business meeting with someone who kept glancing at his or her watch? Are they communicating? You bet.

Did you ever know someone who consistently show up 30 or 40 minutes late? Is that communication? Of course.

Ever tell somebody you were going to do something and then not do it? Think you're not communicating? You're wrong.

Thumbs Up!

I really believe there has never been a greater window of opportunity for corporate America to mobilize its resources and reignite the fires of enthusiasm and conviction that brought us to the position of global leadership in just a half century. The American workforce has both the desire and ability to meet these new challenges if their corporate leaders will unlock their potential that is there and empower their employees to do what they know has to be done.

A true leader is not someone who gets their employees to do what the leader wants them to do. A true leader is one who causes the employees to *want* to do what he or she wants them to do. You don't lead by edict, but by persuasion.

I'm not talking about big bucks to the bottom line. I'm not talking about the bonus check or the wages or the working conditions. I'm talking about the power of a *thumbs up*. I'm talking about the pat on the back. The look in the eye. I'm talking about the "thank you's." If you want to unlock the potential, you just need to let them know how important they are to you. Then just watch that bottom line!

Every single one of your employees needs to be made to feel that they are appreciated, needed and respected . . . just like you.

That's why, on the cover of this book, you see me giving you the thumbs up. That's my message. I think you're the greatest. In fact, every time I speak, I end my talk with the words . . . *You're the greatest!* Then, I give my audience the thumbs up. They love it!

That's the message of this book. That's how I feel about you. Somebody gives you a thumbs up, you feel you're okay. You've just been validated.

You, too, have that power to validate. I hope you will

put that into practice and figuratively, if not physically, give the thumbs up to your employees. To really increase productivity, validate them by walking through the work areas, looking them in the eye, and giving them the thumbs up.

I Feel Good About Me When I'm Around You

The greatest compliment you can ever receive is for someone to say, *I feel good about me when I'm around you.* You'll never forget those words. That's become one of my personal and professional goals with everyone with whom I come in contact. That sums up all of the action steps we shared earlier: listening, understanding, asking, and validating.

We need to be aware of the role we play in how people determine how they feel about themselves. Remember, the greatest thing that anyone can say to you is, "I feel good about me when I'm around you."

I feel good about me, boss, when I'm around you. I feel good about me, Dad, when I'm around you. I feel good about me, sweetheart, when I'm around you.

So here's the critical question. How do people feel when they're around you? If your reply is not good, you're missing the boat. You need to wake up and do whatever you have to do to change your leadership behavior. Period.

Who is it who has a lot to say about how people feel about themselves when they're around you?

You do.

At the same time, you're also going to be responsible

for increased productivity and earnings. If you learn to validate the people who work for you, to sneak up on them and catch them doing something right, these *people who feel good about themselves will produce good results.*

When you make your employees feel good about themselves, they're going to do everything they possibly can to make you succeed. It all goes straight to the bottom line.

Don't be surprised to begin hearing more compliments on your employees and your company than you've ever heard before. Why? Because your employees are making your customers feel good about *themselves.* In an era when customers are ignored and depersonalized, do you think it would impact your business if they felt validated every time they came in contact with your employees?

Definitely.

Customer loyalty is vital to your business. Our research shows that 90 percent of the customers you lose leave because of an attitude of indifference by at least one (or more) of your employees. You cannot feel indifferent and validated at the same time. It doesn't cost a dime to validate your customers, but it has a direct impact on the income and revenue of the corporation, repeat business, and the retention of your employees.

Caring Is Not a Photo-Op

In their book, *Contented Cows Give Better Milk,* Bill Catlette and Richard Hadden drive home the point of how to maintain employee and customer retention:

According to Tommy Lasorda, former manager of the Los Angeles Dodgers, the wise manager goes out of his or her way on a regular basis to let people know how important they are.

"I want my players to know that I appreciate what they do for me. I want them to know that I depend on them. When you, as a leader of people, are naïve enough to think that you, not your players, won the game, then you're in bad shape."
No doubt, that's one of the reasons Lasorda was frequently the first one out of the dugout to congratulate his players for making the big play.

As former America West CEO Mike Conway put it,
"It's not that complicated. First, you've got to care, and then you've got to demonstrate that you care by your actions, because there is a natural skepticism out there. It's just not that complicated, but you've got to be committed to caring.
In July of 1996, we met Angela Perry, a seven year Delta flight attendant, who echoed the exact sentiment, but from an employee's perspective.
"It all comes down to whether or not we believe our management cares. If they do, we'll bend over backwards to look out for the company and our customers."

Herb Kelleher, CEO of Southwest Airlines, put it this way,
"I feel that you have to be with your employees through all their difficulties, that ;you have to be interested in them personally. I want them to know that Southwest will always be there for them."

Caring is not a photo-op. Rather, it's an attitude that's reflected by personal and organizational principles. Organizations that care about their people take pains to ensure that human considerations are in the forefront of their decision-making process when I've develop corporate programs and policies, or while acquiring and designing facilities, equipment and systems. This is not something that I do some of the time, or most of the time, but always. Even if it's unpopular or seemingly less profitable to do so.

That's the absolutely exciting and phenomenal aspect of treating people right. Really right. And that is, when you treat people right, you make more money. Simple. Business transactions, whether internal or external, don't have to be cold and impersonal. They can and should be enjoyable and uplifting and nurturing and warm and personal and emotional. That is, if you're interested in reducing turnover and increasing customers."

YOU'RE THE GREATEST

CHAPTER NINETEEN

IT'S TIME TO WAKE UP

"IF YOU DIDN'T HAVE FIERCE COMPETITORS, YOU'D HAVE TO INVENT THEM"

I preach the importance of validation everywhere I go. Frontline people need constant validation, because they are required daily to actively participate with customers. They need to hear compliments and encouragement. It's a message to those at the top, because leaders need it, too. The question is, who will give strength to the strong?

Too many companies in America today are sound asleep. They have this attitude that they're entitled to the business, or an arrogance that employees will be productive and stay, and customers will continue to do business with them, regardless of how they're treated. Then one day, they ask themselves, "What happened?"

They learn the hard way that there is no guaranteed *employee or customer loyalty.* They disappear.

It reminds me of the guy who jumped off the Empire State Building. When he goes by the 10th floor, he looks in, shrugs and says to himself, "So far, everything's going just fine!"

The fact is, you're going wherever you choose to go. If you choose not to validate your employees, you better start shopping for a parachute.

It's not a matter of throwing more people at problems. Rather, it's a matter of treating the people you already have as assets. It's a matter of recognizing that the human capital you have is just as important as the capital you have in the bank.

I'm very aware that some corporate types in business are not on board with this "validation" theory. They say it's soft, and it has nothing to do with business. They also don't understand why they don't have employee and customer loyalty. What makes the success of the corporation is intellectual capacity, process, strategy, heart-felt energy, and passion for your business and its people. Each component is important and cannot be ignored.

I realize to some leaders, that's like speaking a foreign language. Job procedures and quantitative statistics are straightforward and easy to understand, but how do you chart passion? How do you learn how to be passionate about your employees?

The answer to this question is very simple. I often hear leaders complain that they aren't as popular as they'd like to be. Their employees don't like them. They don't seem able to positively motivate the work force. I tell corporate leaders the same thing I told my kids when they felt like they weren't as popular as they'd like to be. That nobody liked them. That is, if you want a friend, be a friend. Translation to the work place: If you want more loyalty, more appreciation, more friendship, then make people feel good when they're around you.

How's Your Bedside Manner?

I was speaking to a bank convention not long ago. I asked them, "Are you aware that everyone who walks into your bank has sweaty palms?" Imagine the wonderful opportunity to change what customers perceive will be a traumatic experience into a rewarding experience!

How do you do that? You acknowledge them as a person. "First time here, Mrs. Jones? Are you just moving into town? Want some coffee? Tell me about why you're here and let's see what we can do to help you."

You smile, you listen, you understand, you ask questions, you see what you can do to help. You deliver what you promise. You follow up, and you could have a customer for life.

When Mickey Mantle was at the Betty Ford Clinic, he

received word of his son's death. The clinic received more letters than it ever had for any other patient.

When asked how it made him feel, he said, "I never knew how much I meant to so many people."

You'll never know how significant you are to the people who come into your place of business. We spend too much time worrying about the competition and not enough time worrying about how we deal with our customers who are right in front of us.

Here it is, the *Maguire Secret Wake-up Recipe*. It's in three parts:

Number One: Regardless of who you are or what your job description is, you can make people feel good about themselves. That's the compliment you look for. It's the greatest compliment anybody can ever pay you.

Number Two: People who feel good about themselves produce good results. Help your employees produce by letting them know you are proud of them and believe in them.

CEOs are becoming more aware of this fact. If I feel good about me, I'm going to be more productive. Productivity equals profitability.

Number Three: When your employees feel better about themselves, they produce better results. Your *employees will treat your customers better!*

You can chisel this in stone, because it will never change. *Your employees will treat your customers exactly the way you treat them.*

The Rule Book

You see, it's not the *competition* that you have to worry about. It's not *competence*. . . it's leadership; And that has to do with character. Management deals with competence, leadership, and character.

I can't claim credit for these words, but I love them:

Fame is a vapor.
Popularity is an accident.
And money takes wings.
The only thing that endures is character.

You don't have to step over someone to reach your goals. There's enough room and enough business for everyone. It's more productive to help others whenever you can. It's also a lot more fun.

We quickly learned at FedEx that the better UPS was, the richer Federal Express became. Excellence causes others to be excellent. If your competition did not exist, you would have to invent them. Competition made us better. Also, it created more demand than we all could fill. What we learned was that there was more than enough business for both of us.

Leaders must grasp that it's not about competition. It's about working as a team, holding hands as we cross the street together. You know, when you hold hands, it's hard to be mad. And you certainly can't slap the person whose hand you're holding.

Don't focus solely on the competition. Focus on your employees. Focus on doing a better job. Focus on serving your customers!

The Devil May Be in the Details, But So Are Leaders

I am not a detail person. I have no patience to fill out forms. I was well known in my early days at the Executive Office of the White House as the guy who hated to fill out forms. I was laughed at, frankly, for my unwillingness to fill out those things.

Before I left Washington, I was given two forms. One was a travel authorization. I was notorious for never filling mine out until I returned from a trip. As a parting gift, I was presented with a travel authorization filled out and signed by another traveler, Alan Shepherd. My destination was New York. His destination was outer space. It was the first time any American had ever been there, and it required a travel voucher.

My mode of transportation was United Flight 312. His mode of transportation was a Redstone Ballistic Missile and a United States naval aircraft carrier. He even checked the box to be authorized for a rental vehicle, in case he needed one in outer space.

The moral of the story? Sometimes you have to fill out the form. Even the folks who have the exciting jobs also have detail work. Perhaps they got the opportunity to do the exciting stuff because they also understood the importance of the attention to detail. When I'm riding on the plane back to my home in California, I want to know that a mechanic with attention to detail checked out the engine. I want to know that a pilot with attention to detail checked the plane out thoroughly. I want to know that a flight attendant took the time to seal and check all the doors.

Attention to detail makes the mundane the magnificent. As a leader, you must be constantly vigilant to what occurs each day. It's in the details. It's also in the people.

You cannot leave either one out of the equation.

Waking Up to What's More Than Meets the Eye

The other document I received was a job application. The applicant was John Fitzgerald Kennedy upon his return from World War II in 1947. It was for an outdoor advertising company salesman. He fills out his biography which was quite impressive to read. You can see at the bottom of the page, he wrote, "Okay, $50 a week, tops. JFK."

It amazes me that he had confidence, no matter what the situation was. He was saying, "Just give me the job. I'll make it work." Despite our capabilities, we're told by so many elements of society that we should be modest. I agree, but that has nothing to do with self esteem. Of the many leaders I have been privileged to know, each had at least one shared outstanding quality. Total self-confidence.

So, the next time someone comes to your office to apply for a job, or a raise, or a promotion, don't look only at their credentials. Don't look only at the credit report. Look in their eyes and see the light. Use your heart as well as your head. You really have to remember when you review that next job application that the person who wrote it could be somebody who could change the entire course of your company. Some man, long ago, hired a young man, and that man went from selling outdoor advertising to being a world leader.

In a Nutshell

If I had to share Maguire's Philosophy in a few words, here it is:

• **Connect the head with the heart.** If you're in this only for money, you're going to fail and be dissatisfied. Try to operate from the heart as well as the head; You'll make better decisions, enjoy the journey more, and live longer.

• **There's a direct connection between a highly motivated, dedicated work force, earnings, and profitability.** Treating employees well is not only the right thing, but it's also good for business.

• **Become aware of your role as a leader.** The fact is, you are a leader. You need to understand how significant you are in the lives of those around you. That goes far beyond management objectives, strategic thinking and budget considerations. That's true for leadership in all types of groups, including your family.

• **It is no longer possible to lead by edict.** You must lead by persuasion. The employees' day is dependent upon how their boss responds to them. You have no right to deprive your employees of their dignity, hope and happiness.

• **Accept yourself.** The way you are is just fine. What you have accomplished is just fine. At this time and at this place, you are just fine. Truly, if everything's okay, that's okay. But, if everything's not okay, that's okay, too.

• **It's not about motivating people up. It's about validating.**

• **And it's about validating yourself.**

• **We carry our treasures in fragile containers.** That's true. Whether your name is Jack Welch or Fred Smith. We all have fears and doubts. Most of all, we all have treasures.

Inside of you is so much more than you realize. What you and I need to do is validate others so that they will realize that they have treasures inside, that they are appreciated, and valued. Our containers are fragile. We get chipped easily; Sometimes we break. Validation helps put these pieces back together.

• **It's okay to be afraid. But don't be afraid of everything.**
What are you afraid of? Failure? Success? Dying? Living? You have lived on this planet how long? Why are you frightened? Why do you think that after so many years, you're going to fail? Life is a self-fulfilling prophecy. And you are at the right time, at the right place. You are inventing your future. Opportunity is now here. Live like it. Believe in you. The best way to predict the future is to invent it.

• **Live in the moment.** People worry if there's life after death, and spend little time worrying about life *before* death. They are not in the present. Living right now. You can't do anything about the past. You don't know what's coming in the future. You have to live in the moment. It really is a present. Take off the ribbon. Rip open the package. Enjoy.

• **Choose to smile.** If your company is successful, the chances are it's going to succeed whether you grin or grit your teeth. Whether you enjoy the journey or look only toward the destination with no hint of enjoyment, you have a choice for how your journey goes. Even if you are experiencing adversity, you still have the opportunity to validate your people.

It's Time to Wake Up!

Will Rogers once said, "You've got to go out on a limb sometimes because that's where the fruit is!"

When you think about it, anything you do involves risk.

To board a plane is to risk crashing . . . buckle up.

To apply for a job is to risk not being hired . . . knock on that door.

To start a new enterprise risks financial ruin . . . take the Risk.

To enter college is to risk failing ... go.

To smile is to risk rejection . . . Smile.

To love is to risk rejection and hurt. . . Love.

To live is to risk dying . . . Live.

To speak is to risk that no one will listen . . . shout it to the Heavens.

To hope is to risk despair . . . never give up hope.

To dream is to risk appearing the fool. . . Dream.

To climb is to risk falling . . . Reach.

One ingredient I've noticed in the personality of almost every successful leader I have been privileged to know is the courage to take a risk. To try is definitely to risk, but what is your alternative? To do nothing, have nothing, and be nothing. You've avoided failure but you also avoided success.

I have a philosophy. Anything that doesn't break you makes you stronger. In my personal life, I have learned this principle the hard way. The great tests of life reveal character.

What's the alternative to trying? Not trying. I'll take giving it a shot, swinging for the bleachers, going for the win. Life's too short not to follow your heart and your dreams.

It's all in how you see it. We've talked about the word *nowhere*. It can mean *no where* or *now here*. Consider impossible. It can mean *impossible* or *I'm possible*. It's all in how you see it.

Do you see a setback as a catastrophe or an opportunity? It's a matter of your opinion. It's all in how you see it. You can see change as a threat or as a window of opportunity, in which we should jump in, not bail out. Opportunity will always be here for those who are willing to see it. You can see yourself as a captive or a captain of your future. Believe the best way to predict the future is to invent it, and the journey has just begun.

That's not the call to retreat. That's your alarm clock. See your opportunity. Believe in yourself. Don't be afraid. Pursue your dream. It's time to *wake up!*

YOU'RE THE GREATEST

· **CHAPTER TWENTY** ·

THE 3 ESSENTIAL
INGREDIENTS

"GREAT ORGANIZATIONS ARE DEFINED LESS
BY WAGES AND WORKING CONDITIONS
THAN BY FEELINGS, ATTITUDES
AND RELATIONSHIPS."

I have attempted to identify the common elements in the great companies for which I've been fortunate enough to work for. They grew very fast and went very far. Was there a common theme in these companies which caused them to be successful? I think so. They all had three essential qualities. These were qualities which permeated the leadership, work force, culture, and philosophy of each company.

I learned that great workplaces are not defined by wages, technology, the annual report, or even working conditions, but rather by *feelings, attitudes, and relationships*. These three issues, which cost nothing, are the driving forces of every truly successful enterprise.

Feelings
(Catch the Spirit)

Ask yourself, how do I feel about my business? My industry? It's critical to have feelings! You must get in touch with them. You've got to get emotional about this life.

Another word for feelings is passion. Does passion matter? You didn't get to where you are without passion.

I remember meeting Johnny Madden, the former coach of the Oakland Raiders. He has a very memorable way of putting it. He says, "You know, there are three kinds of people in the world:

Those people who *make* things happen.
Those people who *watch* things happen. And those people who stand around and ask, *"What happened?"*
When you feel strongly about what you're doing and about your team, things will begin to happen.

I remember meeting a 70'year old man from Corbin, Kentucky back in the '60s. He had this idea that it might be a good idea to sell chicken in a cardboard box. No way. Not a chance. Forget it. But he had a passion for chicken in a cardboard box.

At the time, I was with American Airlines, as Director of Marketing and Public Relations Programs. The Colonel recruited me with such enthusiasm that I went in one day and told my boss I was leaving.

"You're leaving American? You're leaving the Big Apple? What for?"

"I'm going down to Louisville. Going to sell chicken in a cardboard box."

Suffice it to say that very few of my friends thought that this was a good idea!

The Colonel invented an industry. He was the only person in the world who had a passion for selling chicken in a bucket, and look what happened. We were the fastest growing company on the New York Stock Exchange in 1969.

Not too many years later, I met a 28-year old marine who had just returned from his second tour of duty in Vietnam. He invited me to come to work for him in Memphis.

"What are you going to do down there, Fred?"

"We're going to pick up small packages and we're going to fly them all to Memphis."

"Oh, wow. And then what are you going to do?"

"And then we're going to sort them and fly them to be delivered the next day."

I remember saying, "Fred, that's the craziest idea I've ever heard."

He said, "Any crazier than selling chicken in a cardboard box?"

It didn't make any difference that we had no money. Federal Express, that fly-by-night outfit, changed the way the world does business.

Fred Smith was one of the few people in the world who was passionate about small package delivery. He had so many logistical, financial, governmental and bureaucratic obstacles, it seemed impossible to achieve his goal. *Yet his passion made him persistent.* It bears repeating. He made FedEx a verb.

I was privileged to play football with a group of guys about my age. We all worked together. Nothing unusual about that, except our playing field was in Washington and our coach was JFK. That was Camelot. He stood proudly in front of the world and said, "We're going to put a man on the moon."

He redefined the presidency and the way the world perceived us because he was passionate about his visions.

What was it that the 70-year old Colonel from Corbin, Kentucky had? What was it that the 28-year old marine from Memphis, Tennessee had? What was it the 40-year old president in the White House had?

What they had without exception was passion, enthusiasm, and light behind the eyes. They were excited and had strong feelings about what they wanted to accomplish. They had passion.

It's not about how competent you are.

It's not about how many years of seniority you have. It's not about your job title.

It is about desire. How you feel about what you do determines how well you do it.

Until you become passionate about your life, your goals, or whatever you devote effort towards you will come nowhere near your potential. You have to want it. You have to enjoy the process. You have to have the light behind your eyes. If you don't have it, wake up! Once you have found your passion, full speed ahead!

Mediocrity

I had a history teacher, Joe Caruso, at Xavier High School. Each week, he would return our blue books to us with the grades on them. He would first return the books with grades of 85 and up. Next, he'd give the books back to those who made very low scores, the 30s and 40s.

Mr. Caruso would then take the bulk of papers, the ones between the very good and the very bad, and he spread them out like a fan. He looked around the class and say with all the venom he could muster, "I can't stand people who *meddle* in the *mire* of *mediocrity*."

We need not go there.

I can still hear his words, today. I can't stand to see people meddle in the mire of mediocrity. Mediocrity is not acceptable. People don't have an inclination to be mediocre. If you're having people problems around your place of business, don't blame it on people coming to work committed to being mediocre. Maybe, you should think about whether you are clearly, telling them what you expect of them. Where have you set the bar? Can they see it? Do they understand exactly what they need to do to clear it?

Have you explained why what they do is important? Have you explained why your company is the best? Have you given them a chance to be passionate about what they're doing?

Who Are You?

Think about this. We are born curious; we're touching, we're asking questions, we're happy. And then, the more knowledge we gain, and maybe the older we get, the less curious we are and more cautious we become. We become "professional" and lose touch with who we are.

Too many of us close our eyes for the last time without ever having lived who we are.

We spend too much time asleep at the wheel. We are not aware of what's going on around us. We see people as we are, not as they are. The solution comes from getting inside your heart, getting inside the silence, trusting that inner voice and, instead of criticizing people, validating them. Accepting them as they are.

Have you ever said, "If I had only realized, I would have done that differently." You were asleep at the wheel.

The message is not in the process. We've got the Total Quality Management process, the Just-In-Time inventory process, we've got the Malcolm Baldrige and ISO 9000 processes. Enough with the process. You want a process? Go buy a book. It will give you step one, two, three, four, five and you've got the process.

It's time for passion. For feelings. For validation.

Business Week reported that the typical American factory in the 80s invested a staggering 20 to 25% of its operating budget to simply find and fix mistakes! Isn't that amazing? That is to say that as many as a fourth of all factory workers didn't make anything; They just re-did what wasn't done right the first time. Add to that the expense of repairing or replacing the flawed products that entered the market and the cost of ignoring quality approached, a third of production costs.

The late Ako Morita, chairman and co-founder of Sony Corporation, made an interesting observation in 1986: "American companies have either shifted output to low-wage countries or come to buy parts and assembled products from countries like Japan that can make *quality* products at low prices. The result is a *hollowing* of American Industry. The U.S. is abandoning its status as an industrial power.

We are not taking away your manufacturers' business. *They are giving it up. "*

That was then. This is now. We've caught up technologically. Our quality is good. What's missing today is passion. A passion for life. A passion for work.

It's not the technical part of a job that makes it fulfilling. Are technical skills necessary? Absolutely! When I had open-heart surgery, I definitely wanted a surgeon with strong technical skills. Technical skills are necessary in every profession from your accountant who prepares your financial statement to the pilot who flies your plane. Technical skills are only the beginning and not the end.

Your CPA has to enjoy accounting must care enough about you to understand your plight and your dreams.

Your pilot should enjoy flying. A pilot should understand how valuable their job is. He or she is transporting precious cargo: moms and dads; grandchildren on their way to see Grandma and Granddad; or Boy Scout Troop 324.

Your physician should enjoy practicing medicine. But your physician should also care enough about you to hear and understand your concerns. I am assuming that you already have the technical skills. This book is not about the process, it is about the passion.

Technical skills do not make your career worthwhile. Your passion does.

Passion and You

On a scale of one to ten, how passionate are you about your job? I will tell you, that if you are not passionate about something, I would suggest that you ask yourself why. Stop and think about that one. You are going through life and have no passions. Is that a way to live? Is that life?

I would also suggest to you that leadership *requires*

passion. A passion for what your company does. A passion for your employees. A passion for your customers. How can you communicate and encourage a passion for your company's mission if you don't have it? How are you going to have a dream come true if you don't have a dream?

You're not in the delivery business or the accounting business or the transportation business. You're in the people business.

The issue is not quality. It is far more basic. It begins inside you and inside me. The issue is heart. The issue is caring. I'm not talking about a concern or passion for quality. I'm talking about caring about *each other.*

I must first know that we're on the same team. I must know that you will support me. That you like me. That you trust me. That you see me as more than the deliverer of quality service. Care for each other precedes care for quality.

Does that sound a little soft? A little mushy? Let me give you the business rationale. How do you create a motivated work force? With more money? Training? Incentives? Threats? No. The only way to have a consistently motivated group of employees, whether you're there or not, is to engender trust, care, and maybe even a little joy.

I'd like for us to have a talk. One on one. You and me. Between four eyes, having a cup of coffee. I think we've been misled by our career titles. You are not a CPA, pilot, or physician,

I am not the chairman, the speaker or the author. I'm Francis, Libby and Patrick's Dad. I play jazz piano. I like to laugh. I'm a person, not a position.

Now, having made that clarification, I maintain that we cannot be content or fulfilled by being satisfied with our career titles, beautiful homes, and luxury automobiles. Instead, we must have a passion *for others.*

A passion in your career that enables you to see your customers, passengers, patients, or clients as people.

Attitudes
(Choose Your Future)

My friend Anthony DeMello once said, "All that changed is my attitude. Therefore everything has changed!"

When FedEx started in 1973, absolutely no one gave us a chance to succeed. At the time, we were the largest venture start-up, ever. But, we had an attitude. That attitude was, *If you ain't the lead dog, the view never changes.*

Look what happened. That's what attitude can do.

What I'm telling you is, *you're* the lead dog. That's the attitude you need. You control your thoughts, and your thoughts control how you feel, and feelings control your actions. If you control the way you think, you control your actions. If you control your thoughts, you control your attitude. And your attitude determines your altitude.

At FedEx, we needed to raise approximately 55 million dollars to launch. We had no collateral and very little money. We got to the point where we considered throwing in the towel. Then Fred Smith, a leader with an attitude, asked, "What is the most important commodity which needs to get from Point A to Point B?"

The Federal Reserve float! We went to talk to them about clearing the float every night. At the time, an unheard of idea.

They said. "Okay, we'll give you a chance."

"Will you give us a letter of interest?" we asked.

"Sure!" They gave us a letter of interest which we took back to the venture capitalists who had told us "no" several times before. "All right," they said after reading the letter, and gave us a letter of credit for 55 million dollars.

Here's the lesson we learned about corporate finance. I'd suggest you make note of it, too!

Rule Number One: When you borrow bucks, borrow big bucks.

Rule Number Two: Then, when things go wrong, you've got partners.

And things do go wrong. In truth, "Murphy" was an optimist. The Federal Reserve had too many checks. We didn't have enough airplanes. We got fired. We went to our financial partners, and together, we decided to go into the package business.

To say the least, it was a very humble beginning. As I mentioned, on the first night of operation, Federal Express had more airplanes than packages. Despite opposition, a group of young corporate men and women in Memphis, Tennessee in 1973 didn't give up. They didn't say, "Oh, well, we gave it a shot." They developed an attitude in the face of adversity which said, "Look out world, here we come!"

The president of one our competitors said to me one day, "You know what really makes me angry, Frank? All those people who tell our call center, 'Send over a driver. I want to FedEx something.' "

We simply put the customer first. We learned two rules of customer service:

One: Never promise more than you can deliver.
Two: Always deliver what you promise.

As a result, we had our customers rooting for us. They knew we cared. They felt our attitude in their heart and made us a success.

You'll See It When You Believe It!

An old friend, Pete Harmon, used to have a large chain of hamburger restaurants. At the time, the Colonel was running a gas station in Corbin, Kentucky, with a chicken store next to the station. Along came the interstate system, and his business simply failed.

The Colonel's possessions were sold at public auction to pay off his debts.

The Colonel had an indomitable spirit. Talk about attitude. He never doubted that he would be successful one day as the number one chicken expert in the world. The night that the Colonel's possessions were auctioned, most people would have felt shame or guilt, and retreat into hiding, perhaps for the rest of their lives.

What did the Colonel do? He said to his wife, Claudia, "Come on, we're going on a little trip." And off they drove to Salt Lake City, home of Harmon Foods.

Even though the Colonel had a single, humble little chicken stand next to his gas station, every year, he attended the Restaurant Association convention in Chicago. He would show up in his white suit and black string tie. Everyone knew he had a very small restaurant in a small town in the South.

At one of those conventions, the Colonel met Pete Harmon. The Colonel liked Pete because of his principles, character, and business acumen. And now in a time of personal crisis, the Colonel was on his way to Salt Lake City to find his friend, Pete.

The Colonel walked into Pete's restaurant and found Pete, sitting down, eating a hamburger. When Pete saw him, he welcomed him with a big smile, expressed his surprise, and asked what the Colonel was doing in Salt Lake City.

As I said, the Colonel had attitude. The Colonel walks

up to Pete and says, "Pete, this is your lucky day."

"How so, Colonel?"

"Pete, I've been watching you all these years. And, un-like the others, you haven't made fun of me. I think you've probably understood that I really do have a serious busi-ness. I just want you to know that I'm here today to give you Northern California and the entire state of Utah."

Pete smiled and said, "Thank you, Colonel." Pete also had no idea what the Colonel was talking about.

The Colonel then asked for an apron, went into Pete's kitchen, and whipped up a batch of his special chicken. He showed Pete and his staff how to cook it. Then, he cleaned off his hands, put on his coat and said, "Okay, Pete, here's the deal. A nickel a chicken." Pete and the Colonel shook hands and "the fat was in the fire!"

What an *attitude*! The Colonel didn't have two nick-els to rub together, yet he could see a huge flood of nickels coming in because of a good product, prepared by Pete's capable employees, to customers. The Colonel, despite the gloomy circumstances, believed in his product so much that he continued to be optimistic, enthusiastic, and confident. Kentucky Fried Chicken was born!

The Colonel, who couldn't hold a job as justice of the peace, a motel operator and restaurant owner, felt confident in who he was before he made money, and after he made money.

Do you see the lesson in there for the rest of us? Despite your present circumstances, you have to remain enthusias-tic, positive and confident. That's how things happen. Your employees pick up their clues from you. If you believe, so do they. If they are enthusiastic, positive and confident, your customers will pick up on that, too.

It's easy to panic. It's easy to take out your frustration on others. It's easy to grow complacent. The challenge for the leader is to keep that fire in the belly. You have to have it. Of course, you have to work at it. Some days are better than others. You need to give yourself time away from work to renew, but at the end of the day, you have to have the spark. It's easy to lead when everything is fine. It's when there are problems that the leader earns his money. A leader can see past the problems. A leader always believes in the employees. A leader stays enthusiastic, positive and confident, in the midst of battle.

Pete Harmon shook hands with Colonel Sanders and agreed to send him a nickel a chicken. Pete didn't honestly think this would amount to much, because, after all, his hamburgers were the main fare. He told me that himself many times.

Two weeks later, however, the store manager came up and said, "Mr. Harmon, we need some more of that chicken recipe."

Pete said, "Did you use it all up?"

"Yes sir. It's all gone."

"Well, don't worry about it, son."

"But, Mr. Harmon. . ."

"I'm glad we sold it. We'll just send the Colonel what we owe him. But I don't think we need anything else from him. We're in the hamburger business. That's why people come in here."

The young manager said, "Mr. Harmon, I don't think you understand. We're selling more chicken than we are hamburgers."

Pete Harmon, today, owns three to four thousand KFC franchises. That's a lot of nickels. And it's all the result of an enthusiastic and confident *attitude*, despite the odds.

Relationships
(The Glue That Holds Companies Together)

I had the honor of dining with Mr. Morito, the founder of Sony. We were talking about customer service. He said, "When I started Sony, I went to the dictionary and looked up the word, *Customer*. Here is what I found. The word is derived from the Latin word, custom, and is defined as *a relationship built on faith over a long period of time.*"

When your customers look at you, they ask three basic questions.

First: Can I trust *you*? Unfortunately, today, that's what is often missing in both employee and customer relationships. When you get to the top of that mountain where your employees and customers trust you, your success will spread like a wildfire.

Second: Do *you have high standards*? To get more productivity from your employees, you have to understand that old Dutch saying, "What you *do* speaks so loudly, I can't hear what you're saying."

How do you present yourself? That's the acid test for your employees. What example do you set for your employees? Bottom Line: That's exactly how they will treat your customers.

Do you want more enthusiasm in the workplace? Be enthusiastic. Do you want higher standards of performance? Give them a chance to fail. Everybody wins when the leader leads by example.

Third: Do *you care about* me? This is critical. Everyone of us is carrying our treasures in fragile containers. We have to be sure that we never forget that we are in the people business.

The era of customer-service is just beginning. If you think the expectations of your customers are going to get any easier, you've got a lot to think about. This is just the beginning.

Even in this so-called new economy, the workplace is defined by relationships. It's the relationships you have with your customers. The truth is that your product or service may not be that different from those of your competitors. If so, why should your customers do business with you? Because of your relationship with them, and their relationship with you. You see, if we base their decision on quality alone, their loyalty swings if your competitor gets a higher score on some measurement scale. People do business with people they like.

Every business has its weaknesses. Mistakes will be made, but relationships help you get through those times. If you put all your eggs in the quality basket, what happens when a mistake is made? It is essential to nurture your customer relationships every day. That is how you weather the storms and create long-term loyalty.

Your relationship with your employees is the same way. Very often, they can get the same pay, same benefits and same working conditions somewhere else. Maybe even better. What they can't replace is their relationship with you. As a leader, you have to work at making people feel good about who they are and what they do. You have to work at letting them know that you think they're the greatest. You have to preach and demonstrate that message to your managers. If you don't do that, don't be surprised to see high turnover at all levels.

Feelings, attitudes, and relationships define your work place. Don't be afraid to ask employees at random how they are feeling or what problems need to be addressed or how they feel about what's going on. Ask them what they need from you. Take them to lunch and ask how they feel about working for you, and *listen*. Look for ways to form stronger relationships. It's a never ending effort, but what huge dividends it pays!

YOU'RE THE GREATEST

THE BEST WAY TO PREDICT THE FUTURE IS TO INVENT IT

"PERFECTION IS THE DESTINATION BUT EXCELLENCE IS THE JOURNEY."

I'll never forget that day. I was hanging around with Colonel Sanders in his barn. I saw an old pot, covered with hay and sawdust. I asked about it, and the Colonel said, "Oh, that's a pressure cooker I bought from Sears. I cooked the first chicken in that old pot. Throw it out. It's no good anymore."

I asked if I could have it. He said "Sure," in a tone that let me know he thought I was crazy. I took the old pressure cooker and cleaned it up. Then I had it plated, put it in a glass case, with spotlights, and a plaque at the bottom. I had it placed in the lobby of the headquarters building in Louisville. It became the center of the corporate culture at KFC. If you walk in there today, you will see this pressure cooker that the Colonel wanted to throw away. That old pressure cooker re-ignited the fire of commitment throughout the entire company.

It may not have meant anything to the Colonel, but it represented roots and pride to the employees. The Colonel? He was always looking to the future, until the very end.
I like this story for two reasons.

One, the Colonel didn't rest on the past. That's why it was just an old pressure cooker in his eyes. His focus was on today, and tomorrow, but certainly not yesterday.

The same is true for you. What you did yesterday should not dominate your thoughts. It's gone. All you have it is today. Celebrate it. Get excited. Today is not a dress rehearsal.

Two, when we have opportunity to honor someone, we should do it. Preferably, while they're alive. It may honor them after they are gone, but it makes a much greater impact on their day when they're alive! That's how you make people feel good about themselves. The Colonel has passed away, and I'm glad that I could participate in honoring his achievement even in something as simple as polishing up an old pressure cooker and putting it in a showcase. Despite his protests, I know it made him feel good to be recognized and appreciated.

Life's Circumstances

Many of us feel that successful people are simply at the right place at the right time. Just lucky.

I feel strongly that everyone, including you, is at the right place at the right time. Everyone, including you, is inventing their own future. Of course, there is a modicum of luck, but luck will follow those who have faith and are creative enough to be open to the future. Luck is a combination of creative energy, positive attitude, having a vision, sharing a vision, and staying the course.

There is always hope. But you must first have faith, faith in yourself. We all struggle. It's part of life. Don't be afraid of it. Each of us must make an act of faith in ourselves every day. Your Creator has given you bountiful treasures. Believe it. Accept it. Have faith in you!

That's why you shouldn't compare yourself to anyone else. This is not easy. Years ago, psychologist James Dobson taught us the dangers of comparing our children to other children. He said, and I agree, comparison is not helpful and can often be cruel to our children.

The fact is that my son is not like my daughter. To compare their grades, their achievements, or their failures serves no purpose. Why? Because they are completely different individuals. It would be just as foolish of me to compare my children with your children.

The same is true for you and I. I cannot compare myself with you. You are either taller or shorter than I am. You are older or younger. You make more or less money. You have a larger or smaller house. Some of these differences are

clear and undeniable. Certainly we can acknowledge them, but to draw conclusions is foolish and meaningless. You are different, and that is what makes the world so interesting. I'm glad everyone doesn't want to be me, or I'd be out of work. I'm glad everyone doesn't play the piano, or nobody would want to hear me play. But differences don't determine values. That's the message I'm sharing with you.
Value is what you place on yourself.

You should always feel good about who you are, regardless of your circumstances. The extent to which you are able to do that is the extent to which you are able to invent your future and your luck.

Don't Sit Back!

We must look at ourselves and say "Yes!" We must believe that we are in the right place at the right time. You determine the way you feel about your circumstances and your dreams. Despite where you want to be, you must enjoy the now, today. That's true whether you're 15, 40, or 75 years old.

Life is how you choose to look at it. It's 10 percent what happens to you and 90 percent how you deal with it. You can look at your life and see the setbacks, or you can see the achievements. You can see the firings or you could see the hirings.

You can see hope or you can see despair. It was the philosopher Snoopy who said, "Yesterday I was a dog. Today I'm a dog. Tomorrow I'll probably still be a dog. There is just so little hope for advancement."

For me, personally, life has culminated in a spot where I have never been happier. Life is a journey, and your journey is what you make of it. It's your choice, right now, how you see it. Yesterday's gone and tomorrow is not here. All you've got is now the present.

It reminds me of an old man sitting by the gate of a city. As a traveler walked by, he asked the old man, "What kind of city is this?"

The old man asked, "What was the city like where you came from?"

"Oh, it was terrible," the traveler replied. "It was full of mean people. I hated it. I couldn't wait to get out."

"That's what you'll find here," the old man lamented.

Soon another traveler came by and asked what type of city he would find.

"What kind of city did you come from?" the old man asked.

"It was a *wonderful* place. They are my best friends. I loved them so much and I hope we stay friends forever."

The old man smiled and said, "That's what you'll find here."

We see people and life as *we* are, not as they are. If you believe you're in the right place at the right time, you will be. It's not luck. It's life. How you perceive your company, your managers, your employees, your product, your services and your customers will determine your reality.

If you believe in them, you will enjoy the journey and thrive. Remember, the best way to predict the future is to invent it.

The Journey Has Just Begun

In March of 1991, I was told by young Dr. Robbins and my friend, Dr. Bill Oswald that I was going to undergo a quadruple bypass. When you hear those words, you think that you're going to die. You really don't take much comfort in how successful the operation has been for others. When you're talking about your heart, it's a whole different story!

I thought I was going to die. Everybody else could make

it, but I thought I would not. I was out of here. I was history. But, when I reached the other side of my operation and I survived, I realized that my journey had not come to an end. Rather, my journey had just begun.

So, it was time for me to get on with life.

When I returned to my home, I asked the question, What is it that put me in that bed? I recognized that I had put myself in the bed by seeking to be a perfectionist. Almost everyone is seeking perfection, and it's so silly.

That to me is the greatest single sin you can commit. Because when you seek perfection, you refuse to acknowledge those gifts you've been given. Everyone one of us, without exception, has many, many gifts. If we stopped to celebrate them, we would have a much more fulfilled life. But no, we continue to press on, to get it perfect, perfect, perfect. As a result, I wound up with a nice reminder on my chest. A keepsake to help me acknowledge my gifts.

Those qualities that define my excellence.
To treasure them.
To recognize them.
To take credit for them.
To be grateful for them.
To understand that you're not perfect.
You never will be perfect.
And neither is anyone else perfect.

But what we need to do while we're here on this earth is to celebrate those gifts which we have been given.
To celebrate our excellence.

Finally, it dawned on me that I was a perfectionist. I realized at that moment that I had failed to recognize the excellence I possessed. So, I sat down and wrote myself a letter. In it, I compared perfection and excellence.

It was so obvious. I'd like to share it with you.

Your Journey Has Just Begun

Perfection is being right.
Excellence is willing to be wrong.

Perfection is fear.
Excellence is taking a risk.

Perfection is anger and frustration.
Excellence is powerful.

Perfection is control.
Excellence is spontaneous.

Perfection is judgment.
Excellence is accepting.

Perfection is taking.
Excellence is giving.

Perfection is doubt.
Excellence is confidence.

Perfection is pressure.
Excellence is natural.

Perfection is the destination.
Excellence is the journey.

That letter to myself really helped me understand that I don't have to be perfect. There is no *perfect*! I can let go of that stress. And let out a big sigh of relief. It's okay not to be perfect. Whew! Hooray!

Of course, the letter is for you, too. Let go. Let out your own sigh of relief.

You know what I did? Quit looking inside for blame and guilt. Look to the needs and feelings of *others*. I don't have to be so worried about how I'm doing. People will think what they want to think anyway. It allowed me not to be afraid to make mistakes, so I've got a little more latitude; I can take a few more risks; I can concentrate on letting others know they're the greatest. Write your own letter, the one you've been carrying around for years!

Life Outside The Lines

Erma Bombeck once said that if she had her life to live over again, she wouldn't be so concerned with keeping her kitchen spotless and she would eat more in the dining room and burn the good candles. She would hug more instead of worrying about the dust on the coffee table.

I think a good exercise for some of us would be to find a fresh page in a coloring book, select a nice bold crayon, and scribble all over it. Go outside the lines. Just let those strokes go everywhere - up and down, from side to side, in and out of those lines. How liberating. Whoever said we had to stay in those lines anyway? What's the worst thing that can happen if you go outside the lines?

Sure, there are some things which require more attention to detail than others. However, most things, short of by-pass surgery are fairly generous and forgiving.

What does all this have to do with your job?

Absolutely everything. If you are tied to a standard of perfection, then you will never be able to please yourself, and neither will your employees. If you don't measure up, how can your employees? Transactionally, you will feel, "I'm not

OK, and neither are my employees, or my family."

If you wake up, so will they. Be the leader you are!

Once you learn to accept yourself, imperfections and all, you become a much more effective leader. Not to mention that life takes on much more enjoyment for you and everyone around you.

Stop trying to be perfect. Accept yourself the way you are. Do your best, and be okay with who you are. Understand that you're ok, and validate others in your life so that they will know how much you appreciate them.

The results mean greater productivity, more profit, lower turnover and greater loyalty in employees and customers. It also means lower blood pressure, fewer migraines, more smiles, more laughs, more friends, improved leadership skills, increased interpersonal skills and a life that touches the hearts and lives of others.

So what are you waiting for? Get in there and do it! But before you go, let me tell you just one more time, for old time's sake, so you won't forget, so you'll carry the torch and pass the message on today and everyday . . .

You're the Greatest!

For information about quantity orders, interviews, speeches, and workshops, please contact:

Frank Maguire
32123 Lindero Canyon Road, #204
Westlake Village, CA 91361

Phone: 818.889.8086

Fax: 818.889.0686

888-437-2656 toll free

FrankMaguire.com